I0491609

Spain
Coloring Book

Adult Coloring Books

Aryla Publishing 2019

Copyright @ 2019 Aryla Publishing All Rights Reserved

No part of this book may be reproduced or transmitted in any form or by means, electronic or mechanical, including photocopying recording or by any information storage and retrieval system without written permission from the publisher

978-1-912675-54-8

www.arylapublishing.com

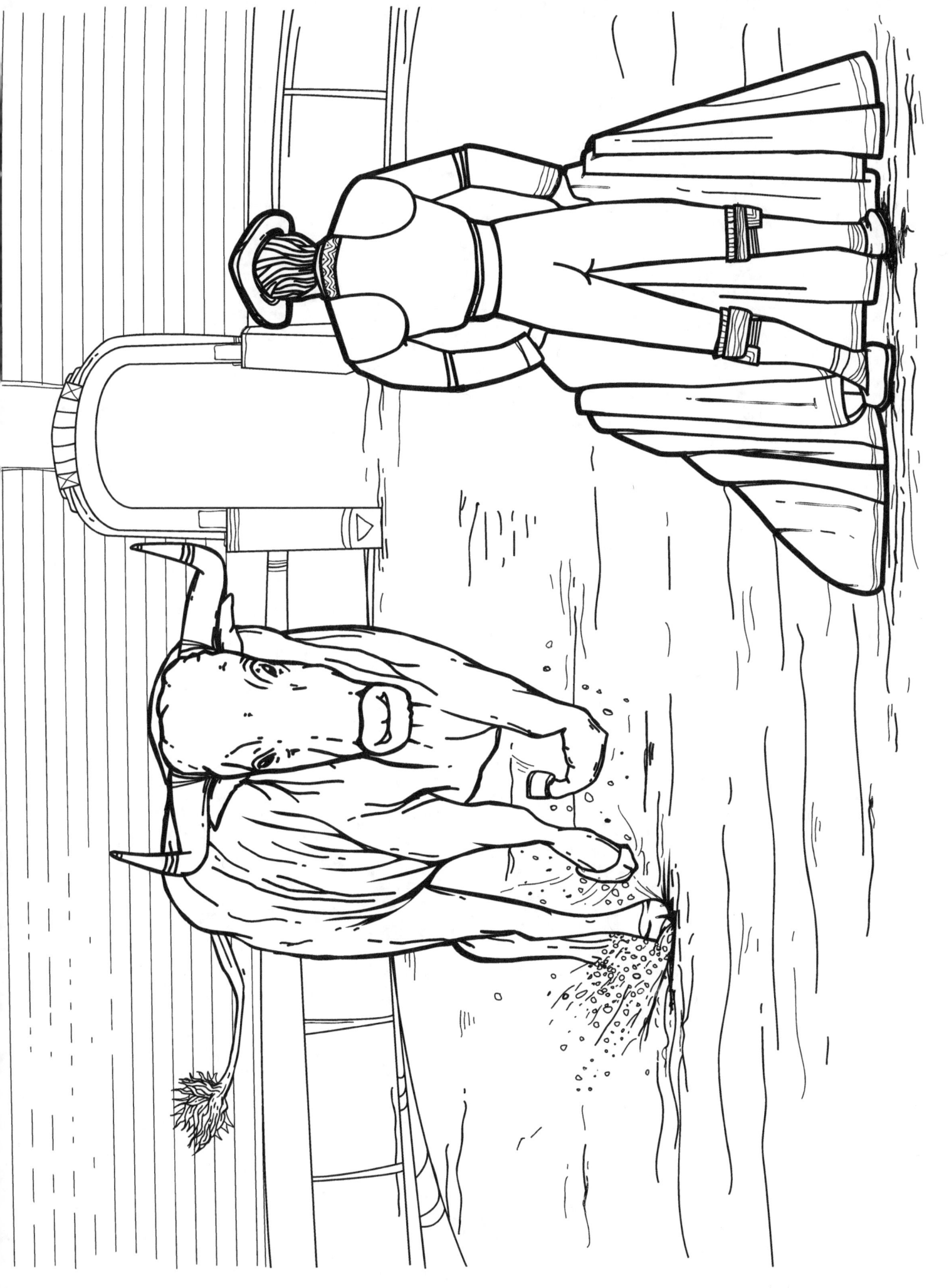

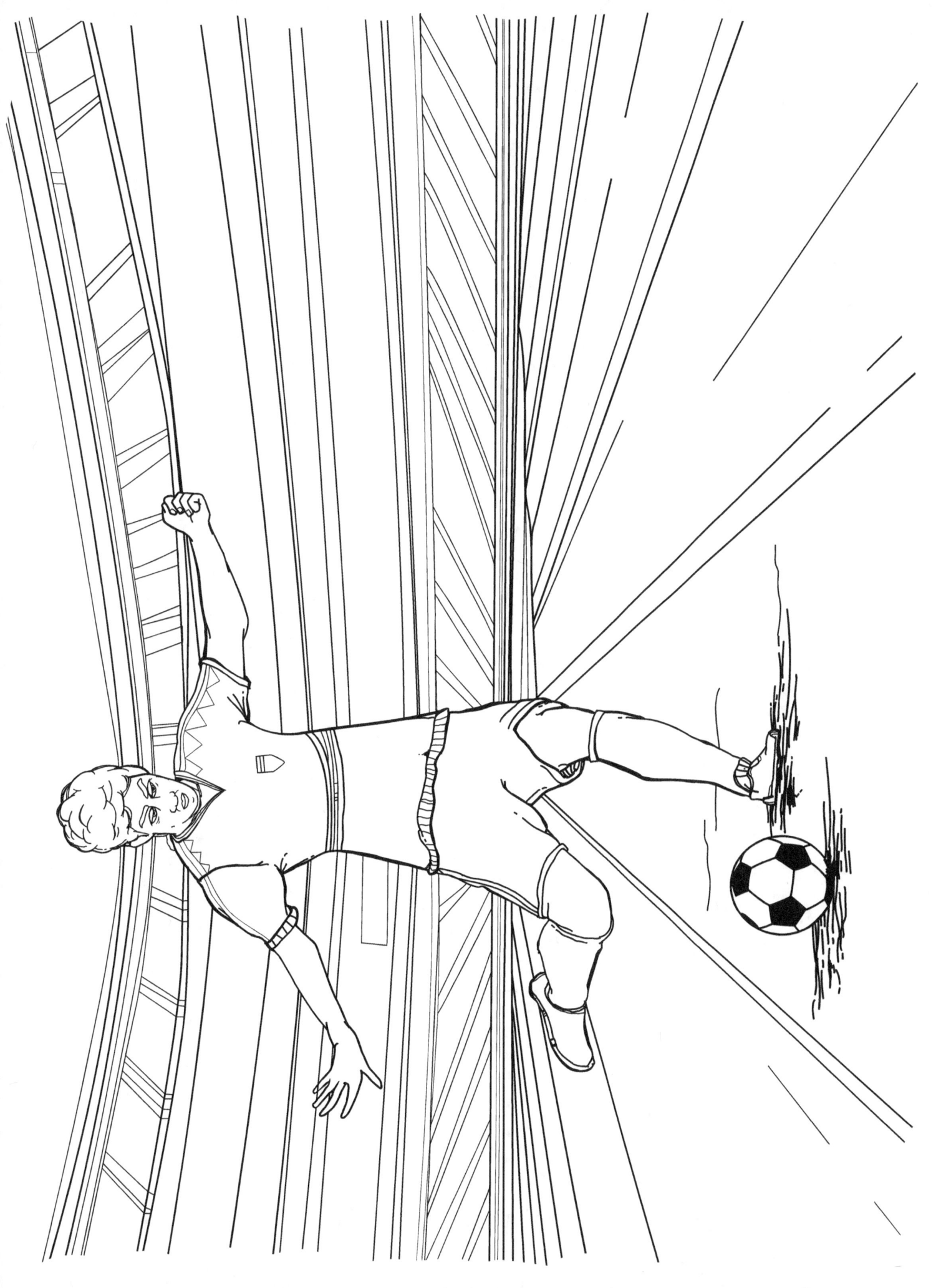

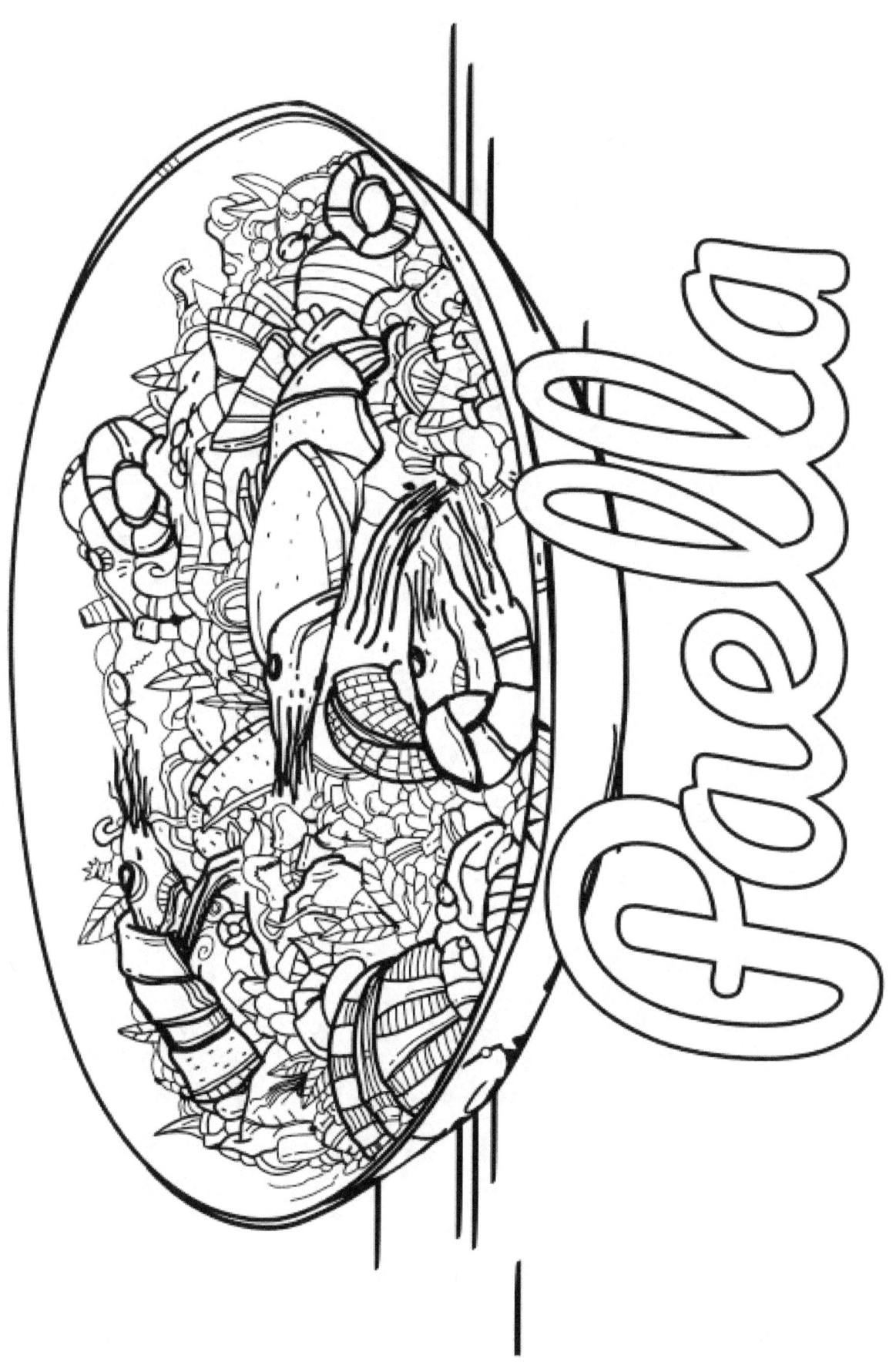

Paella

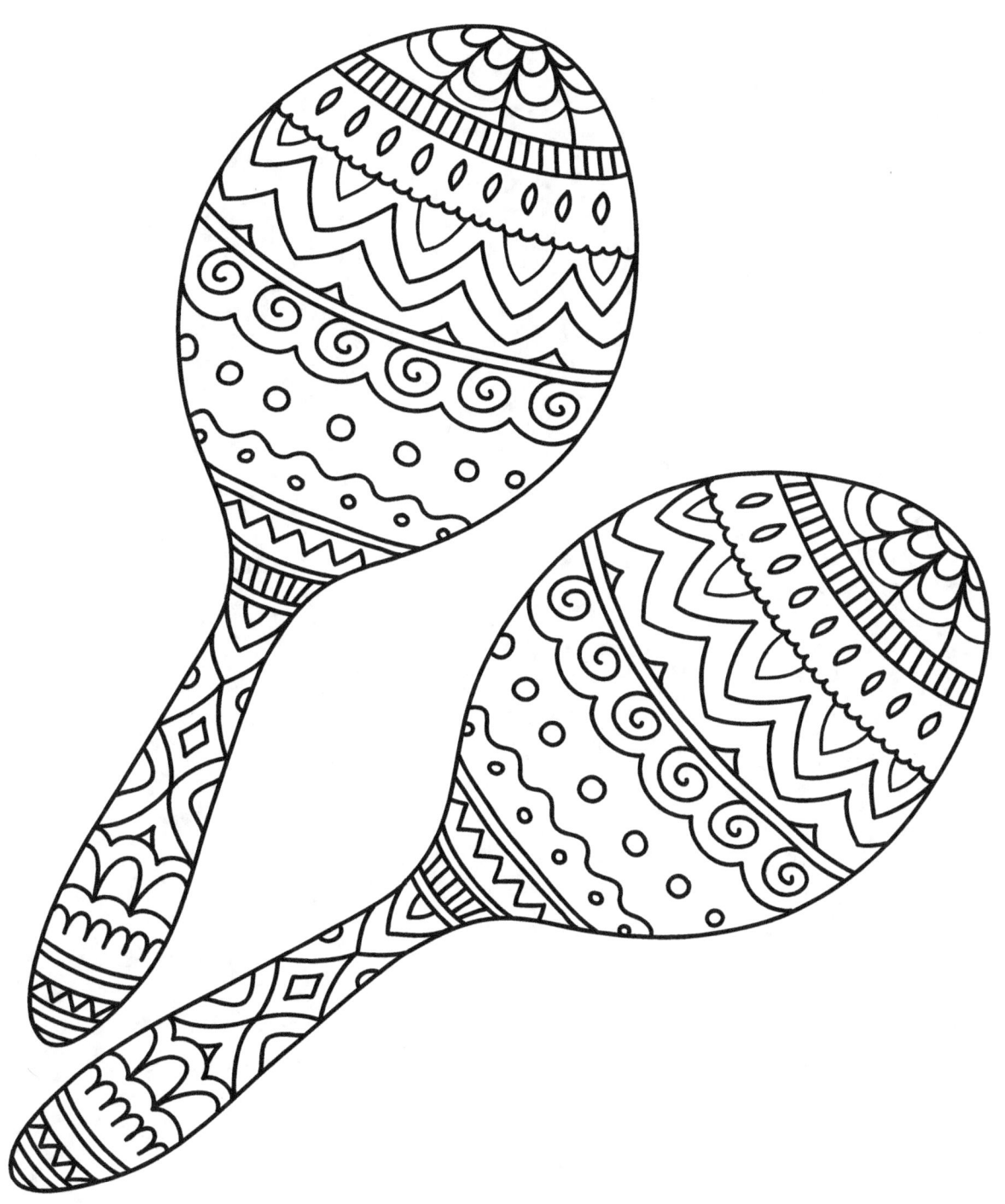

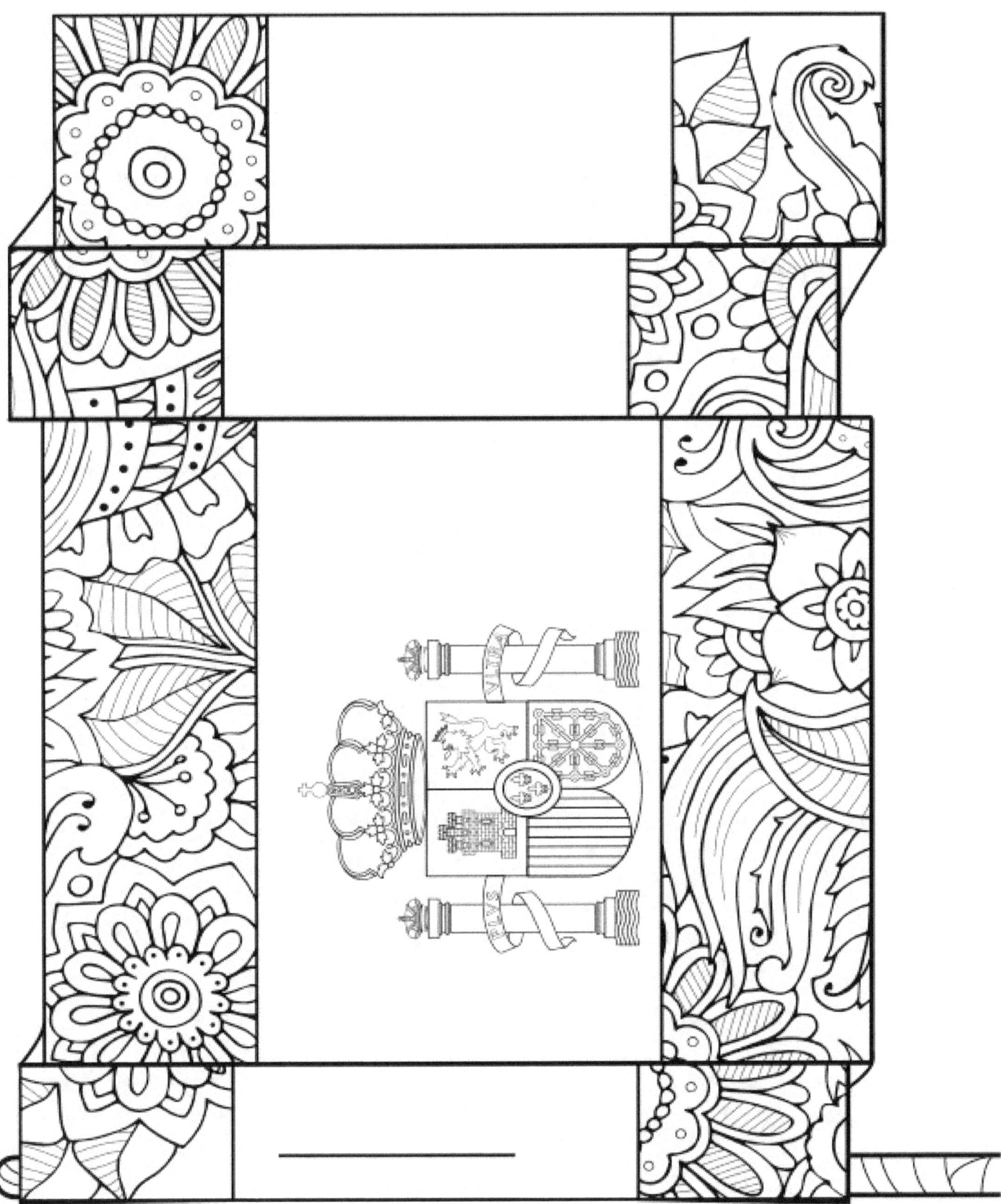

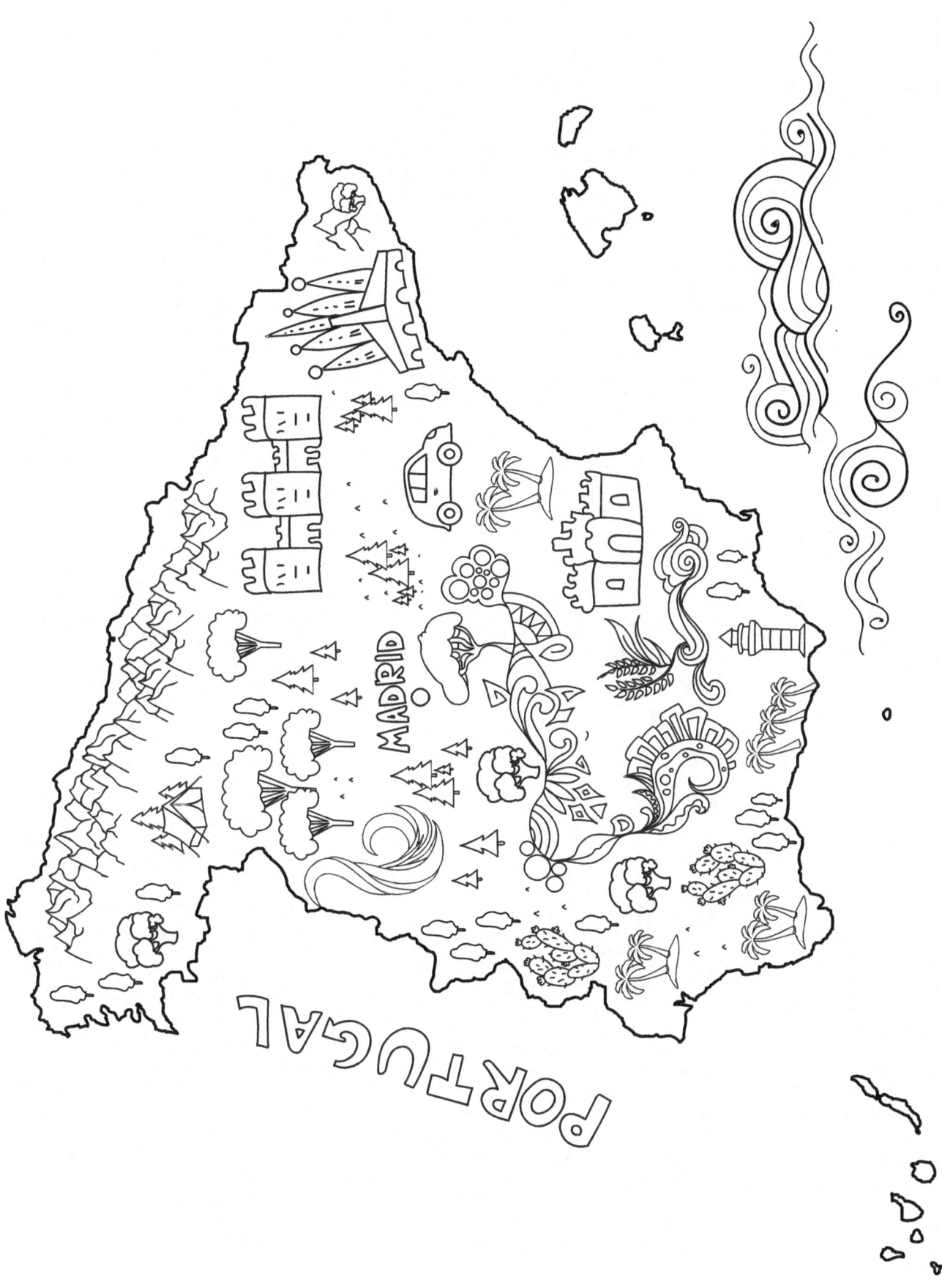

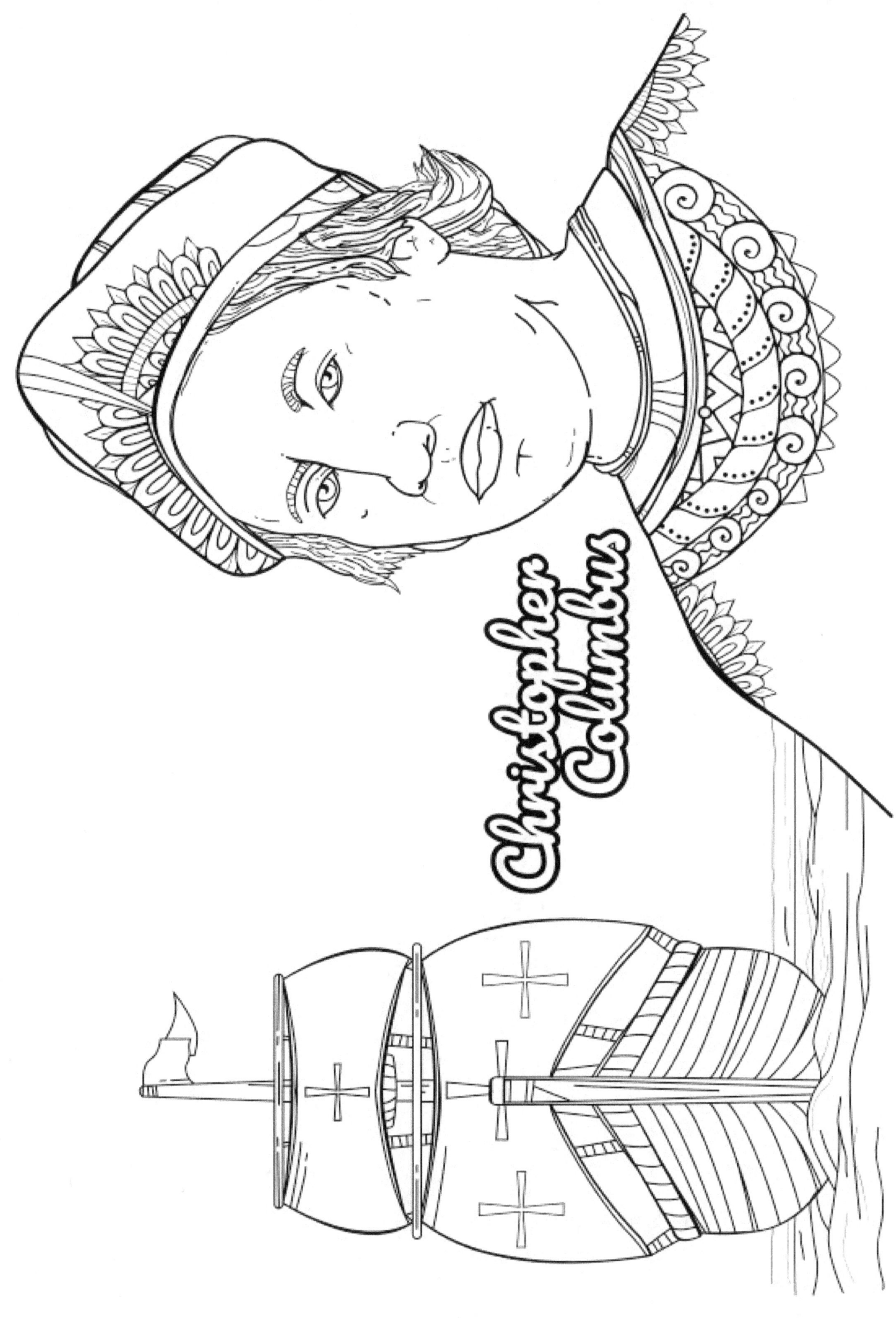

Christopher Columbus

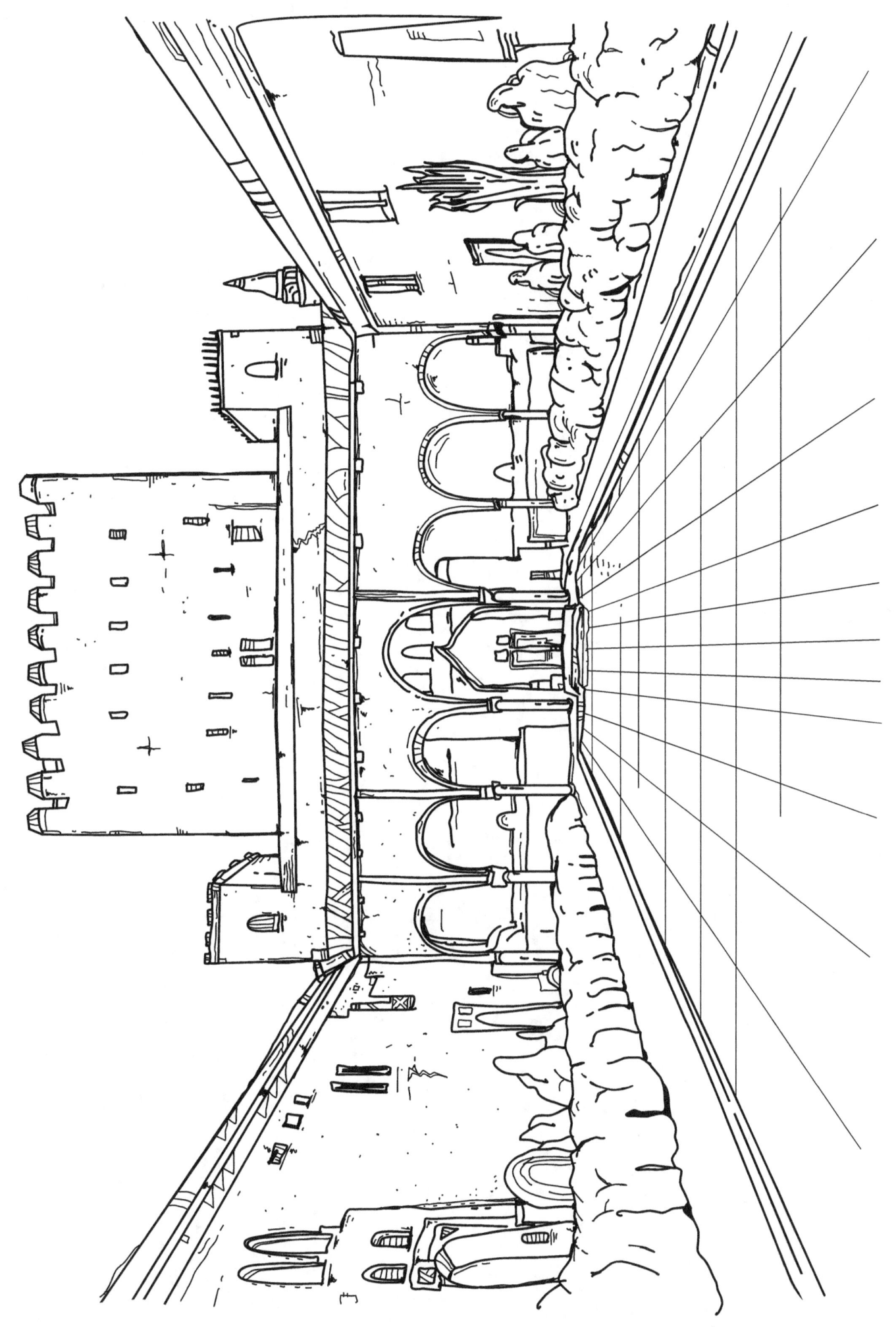

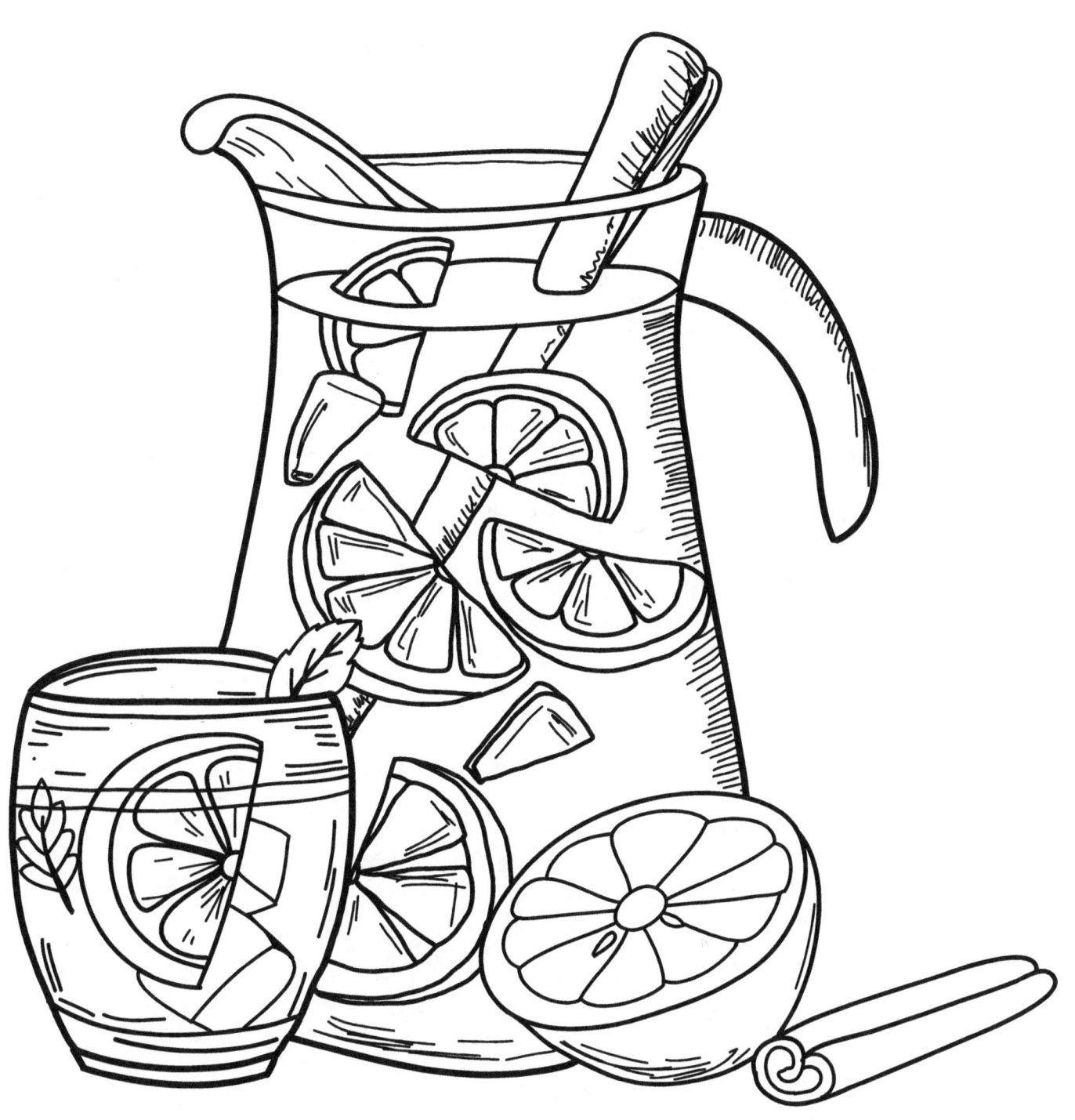

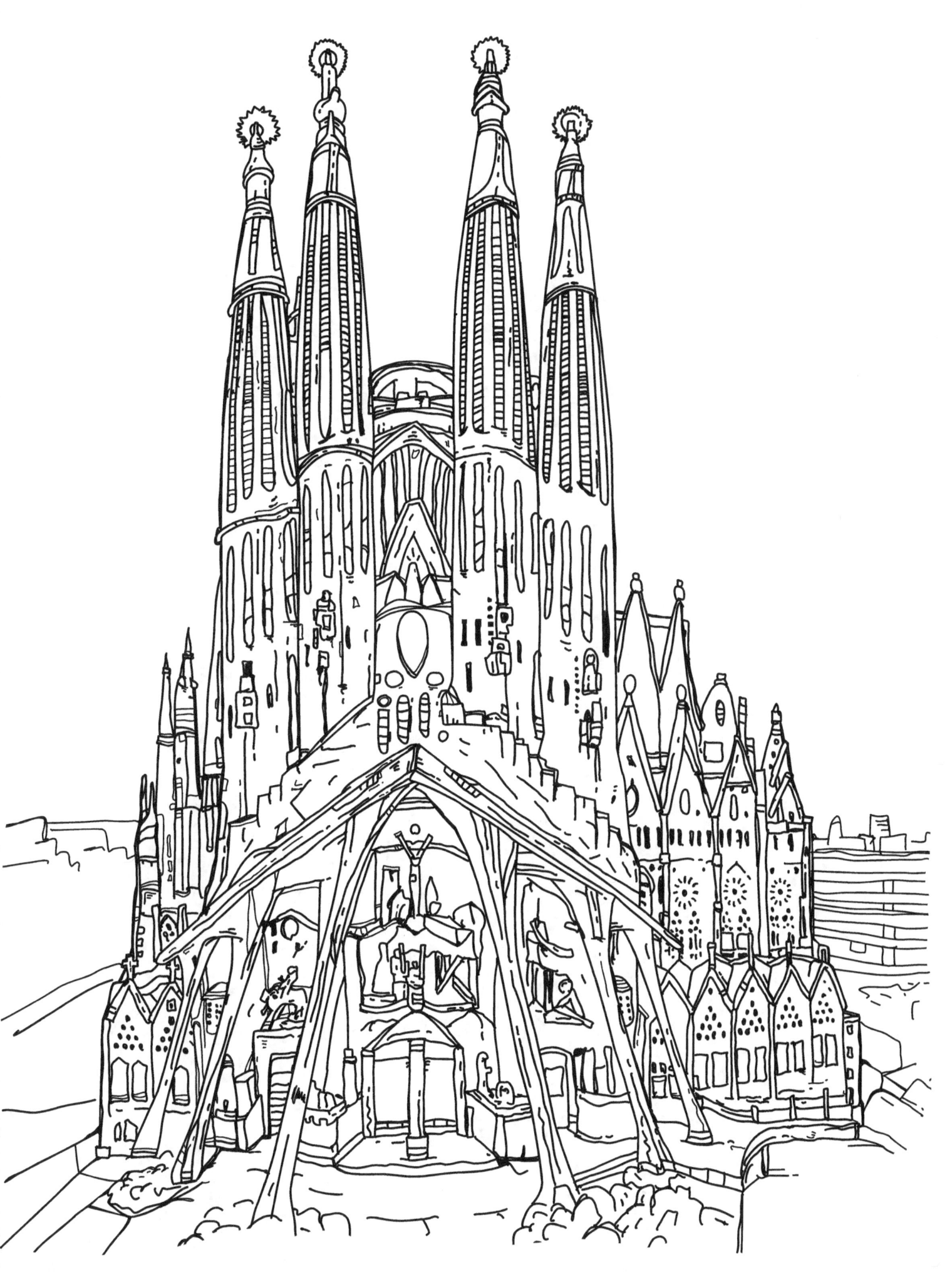

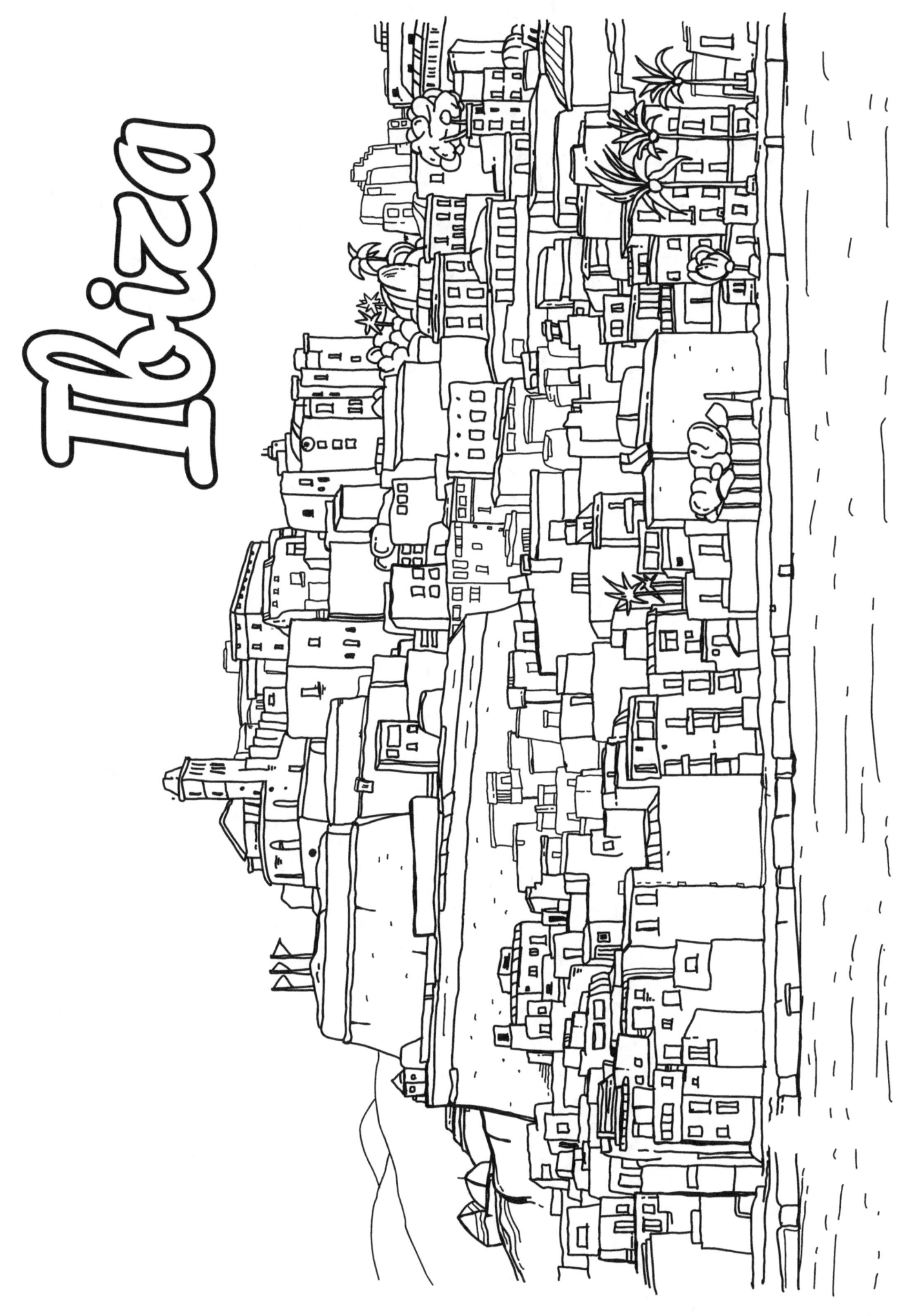

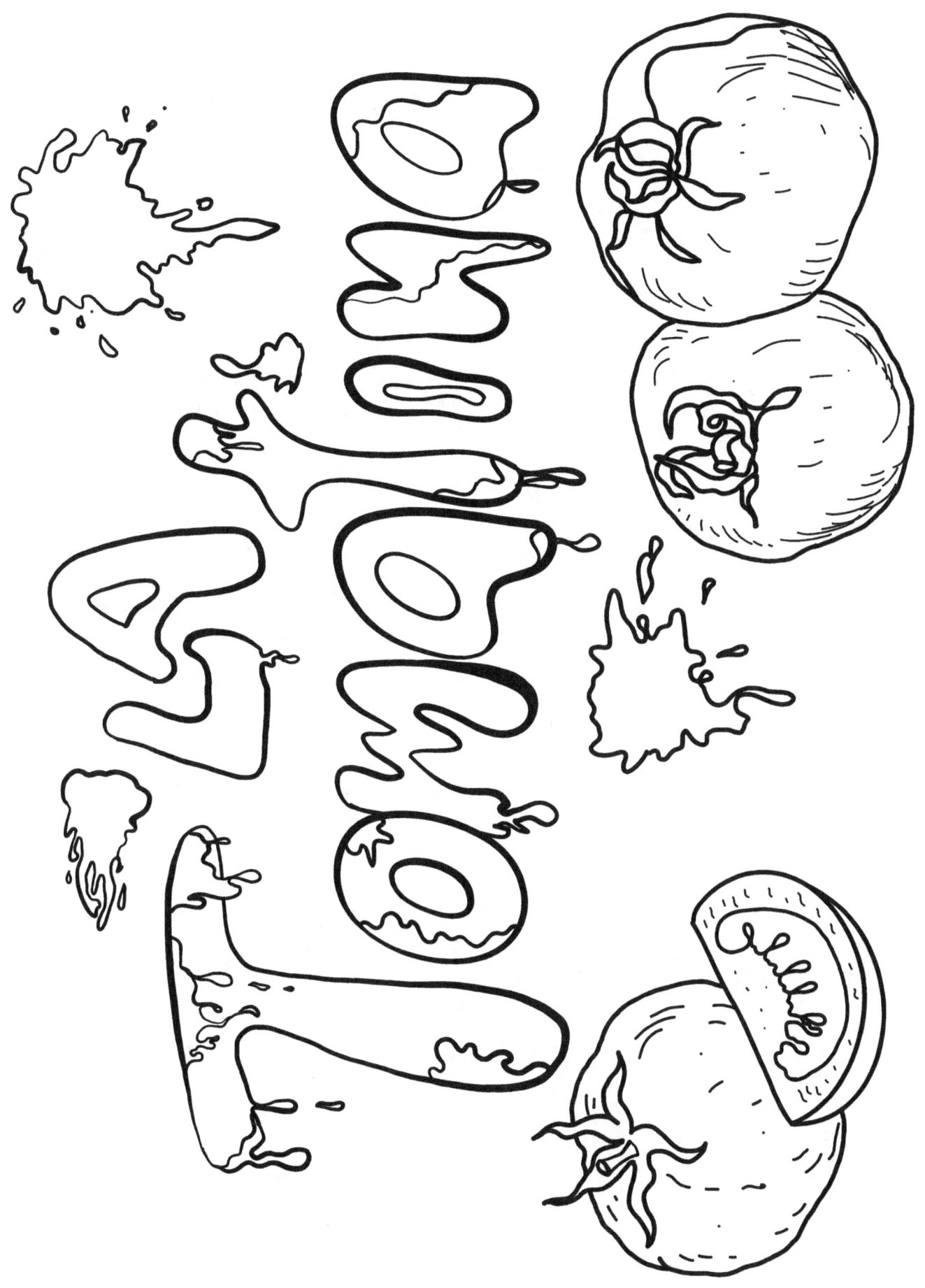

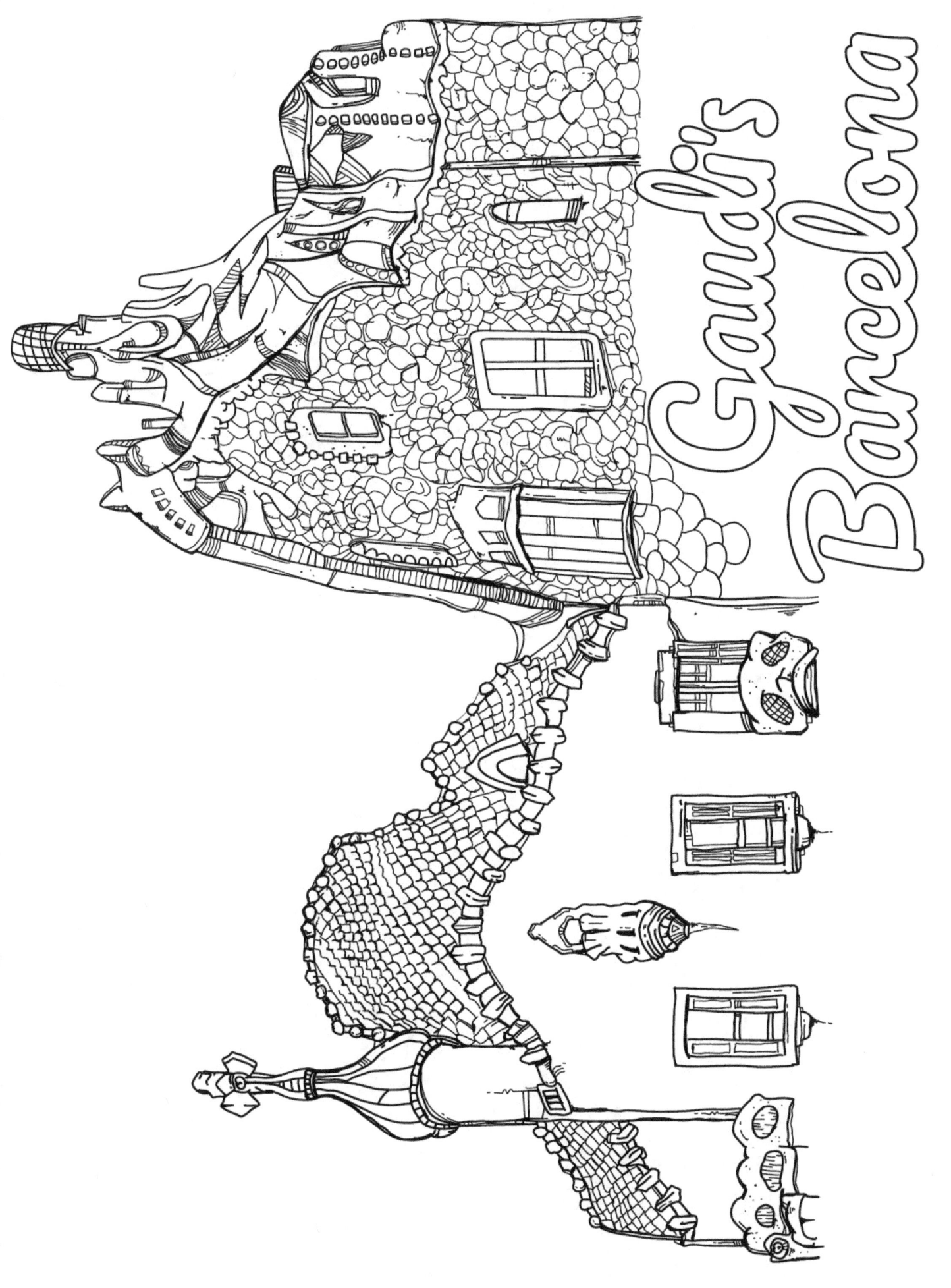

Gaudí's Barcelona

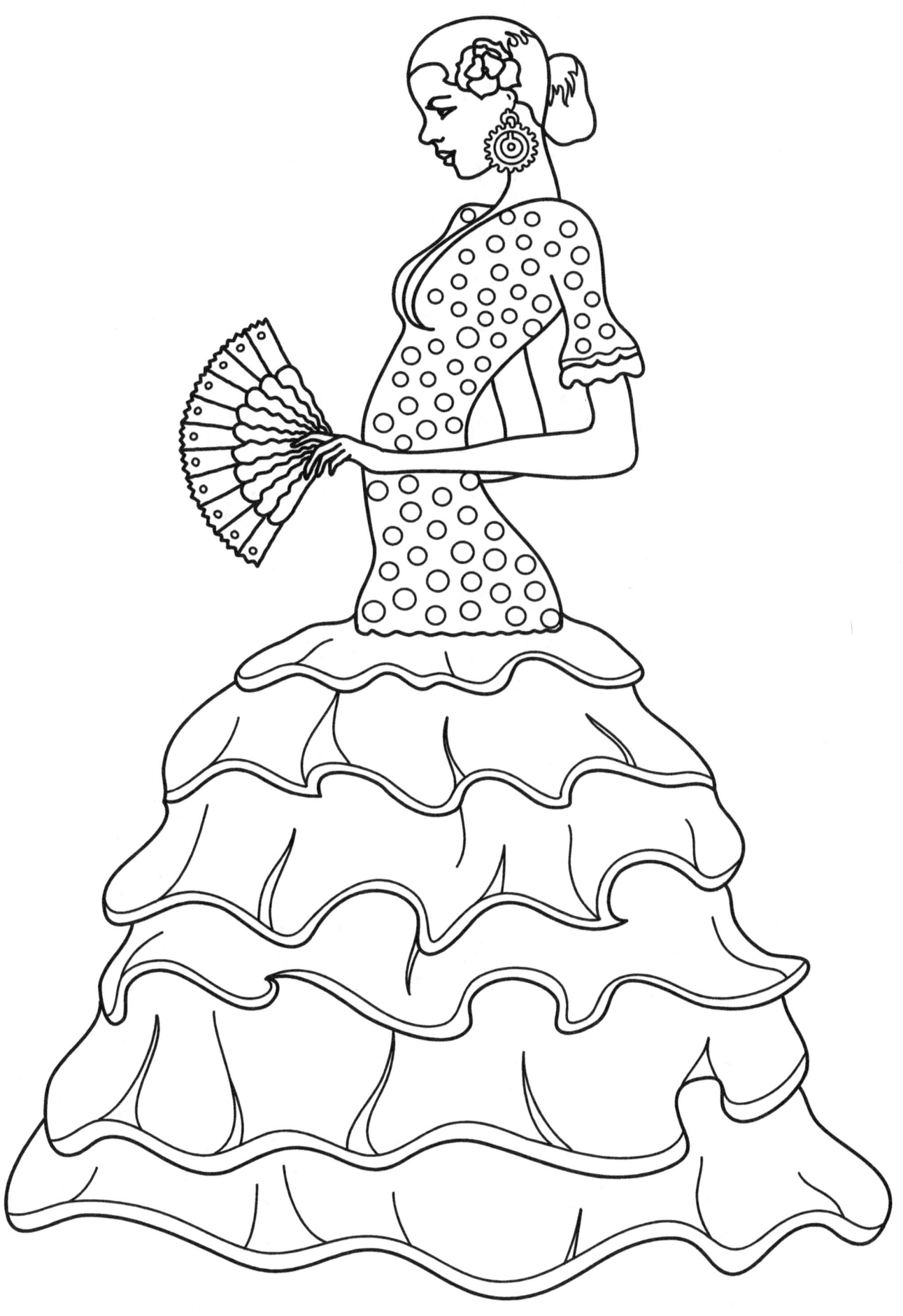

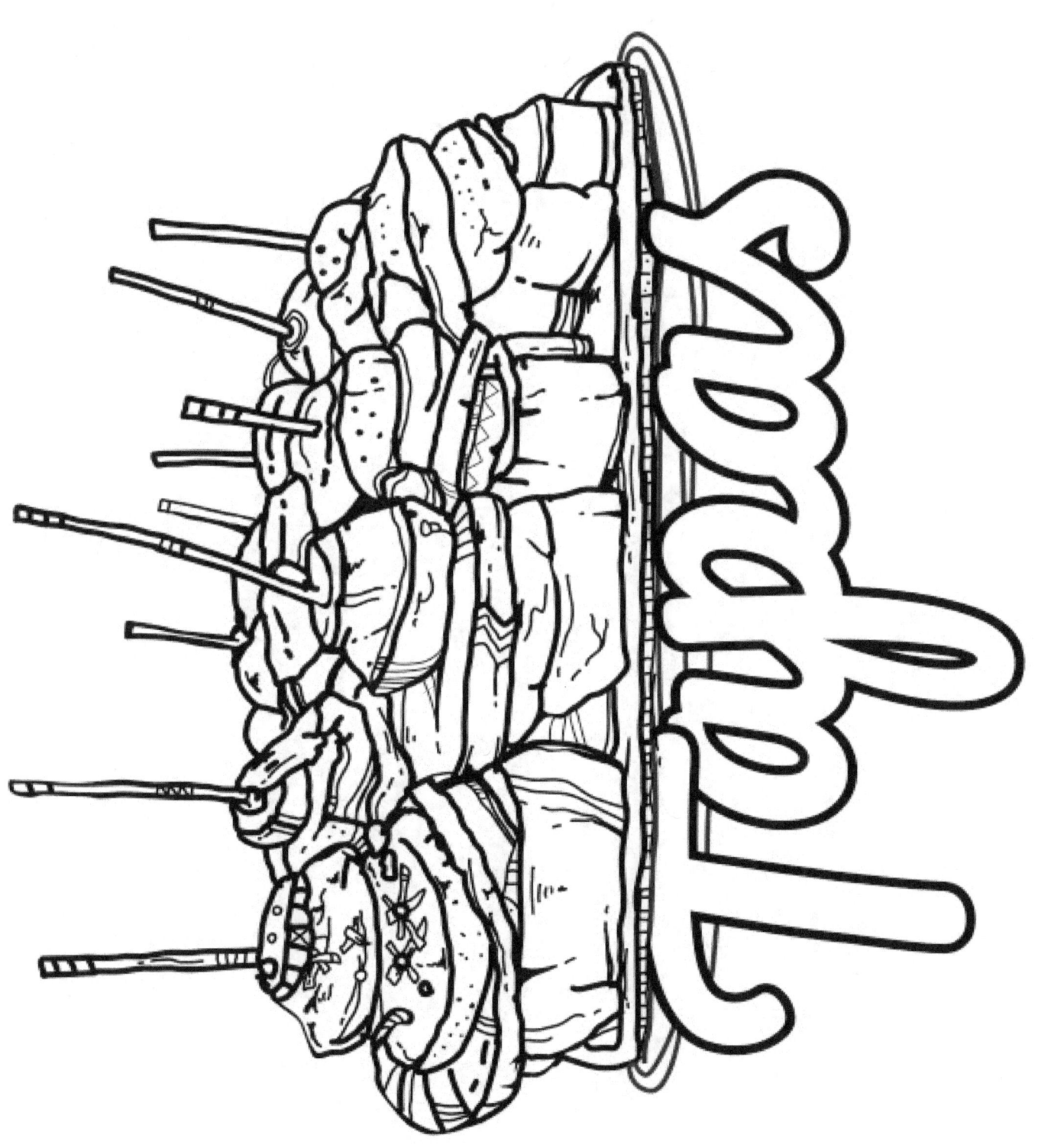

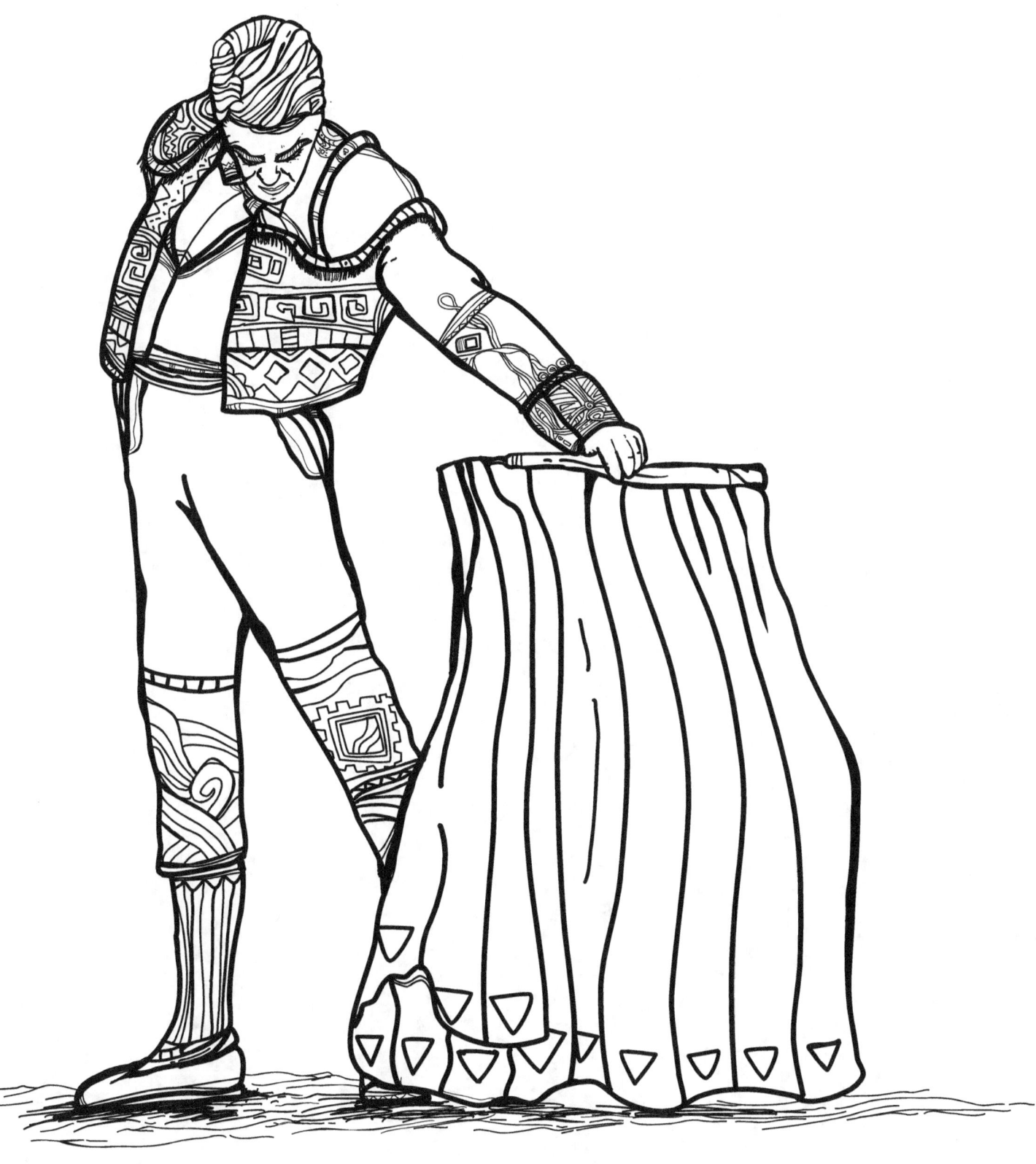

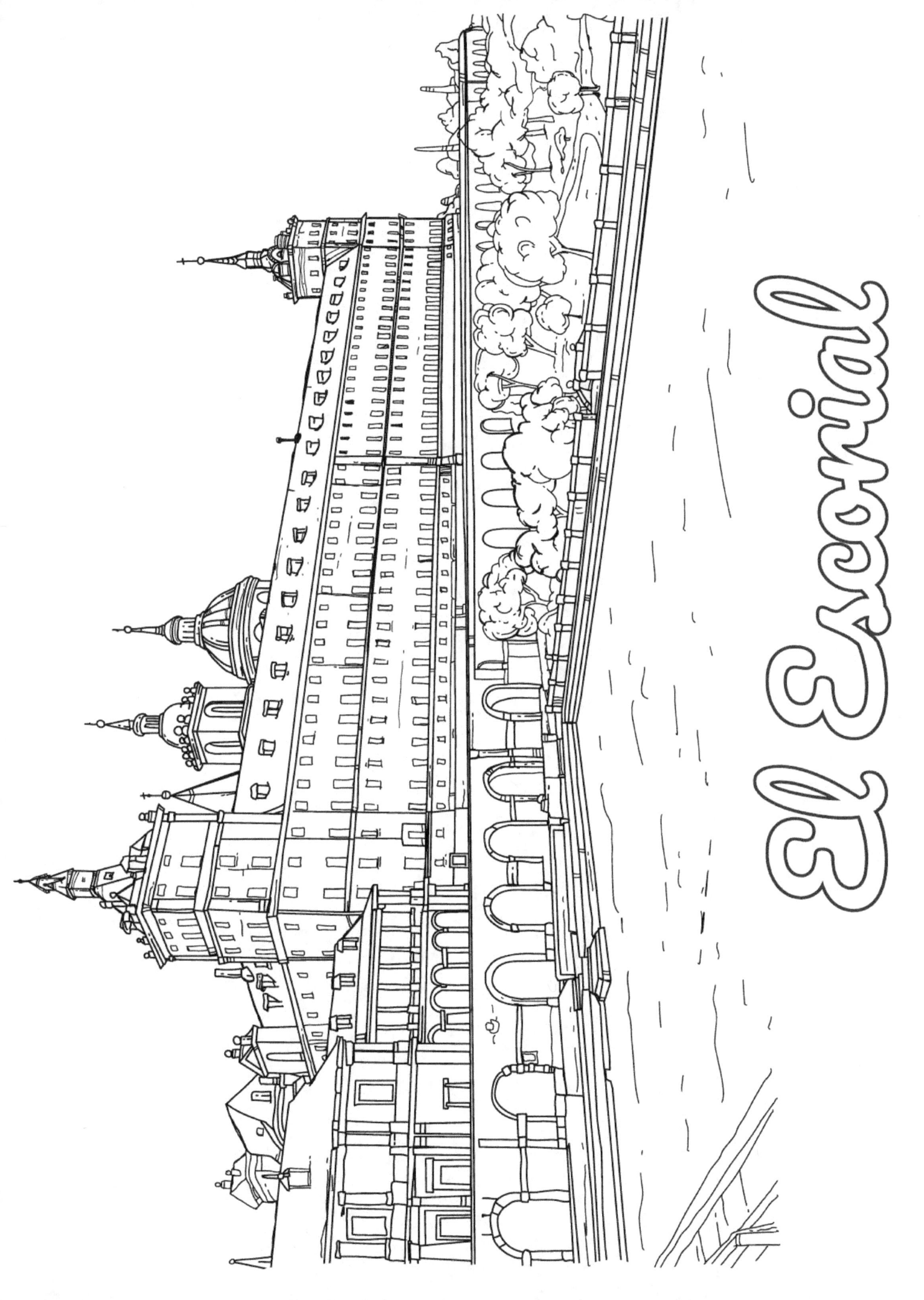

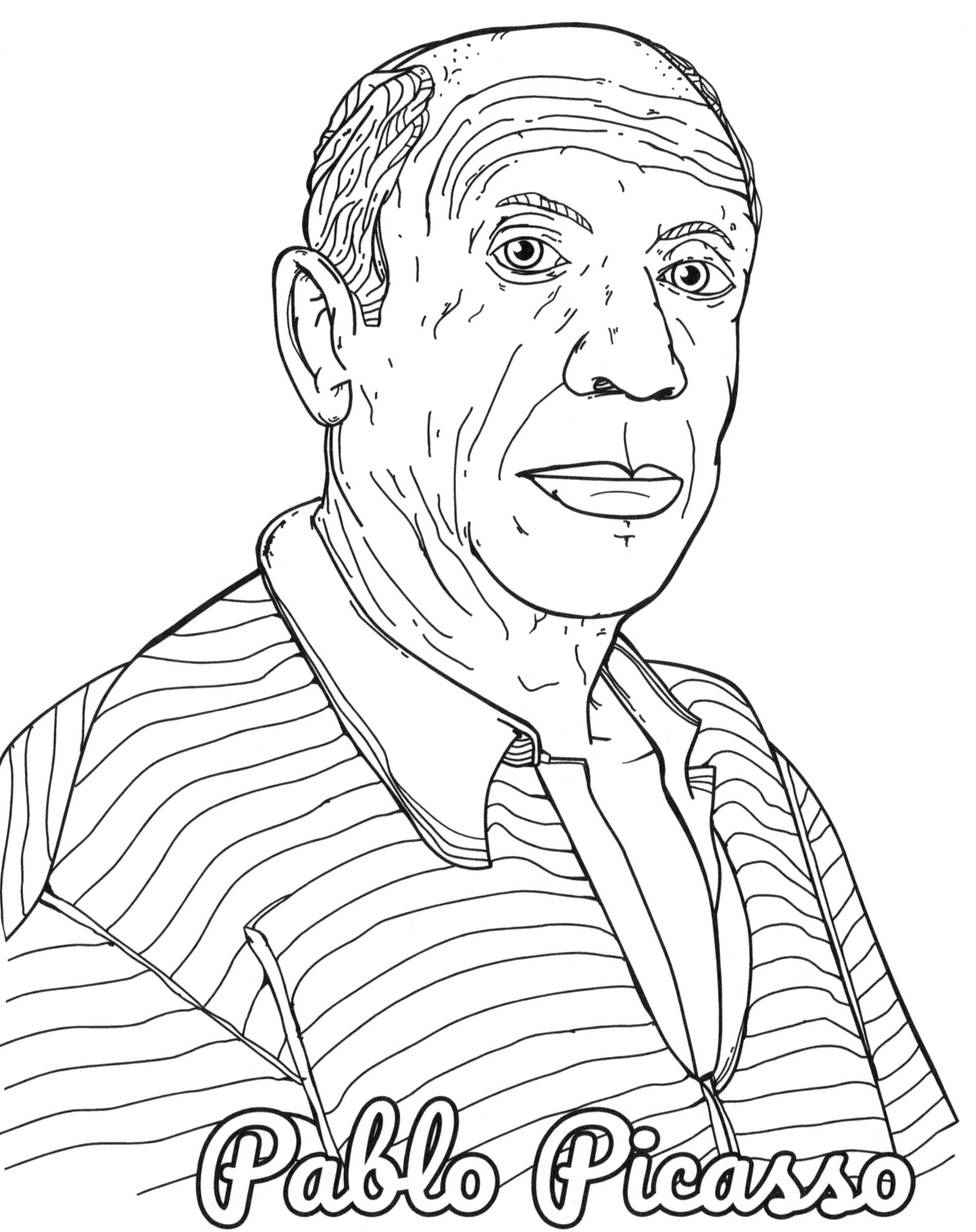

Pablo Picasso

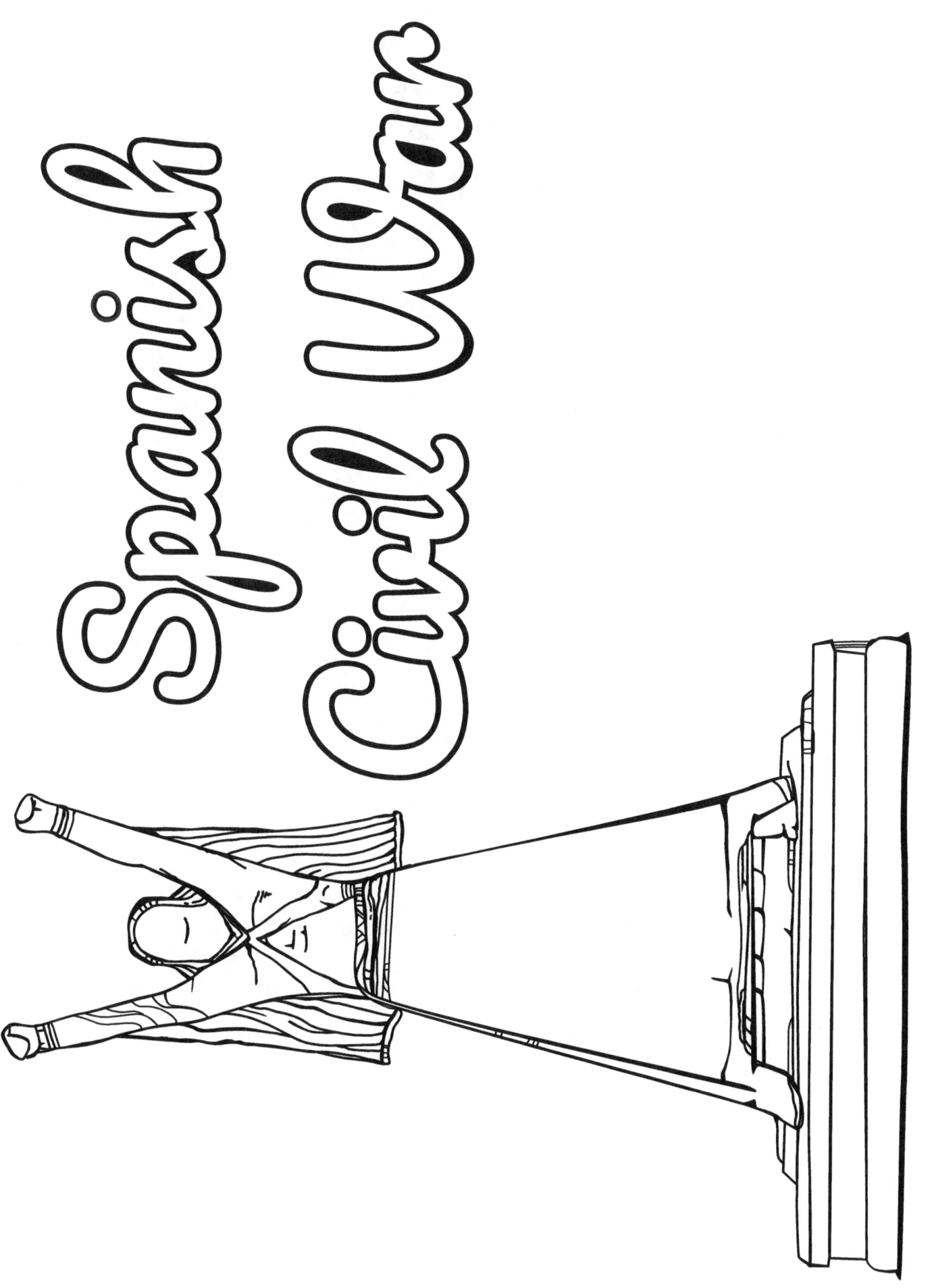

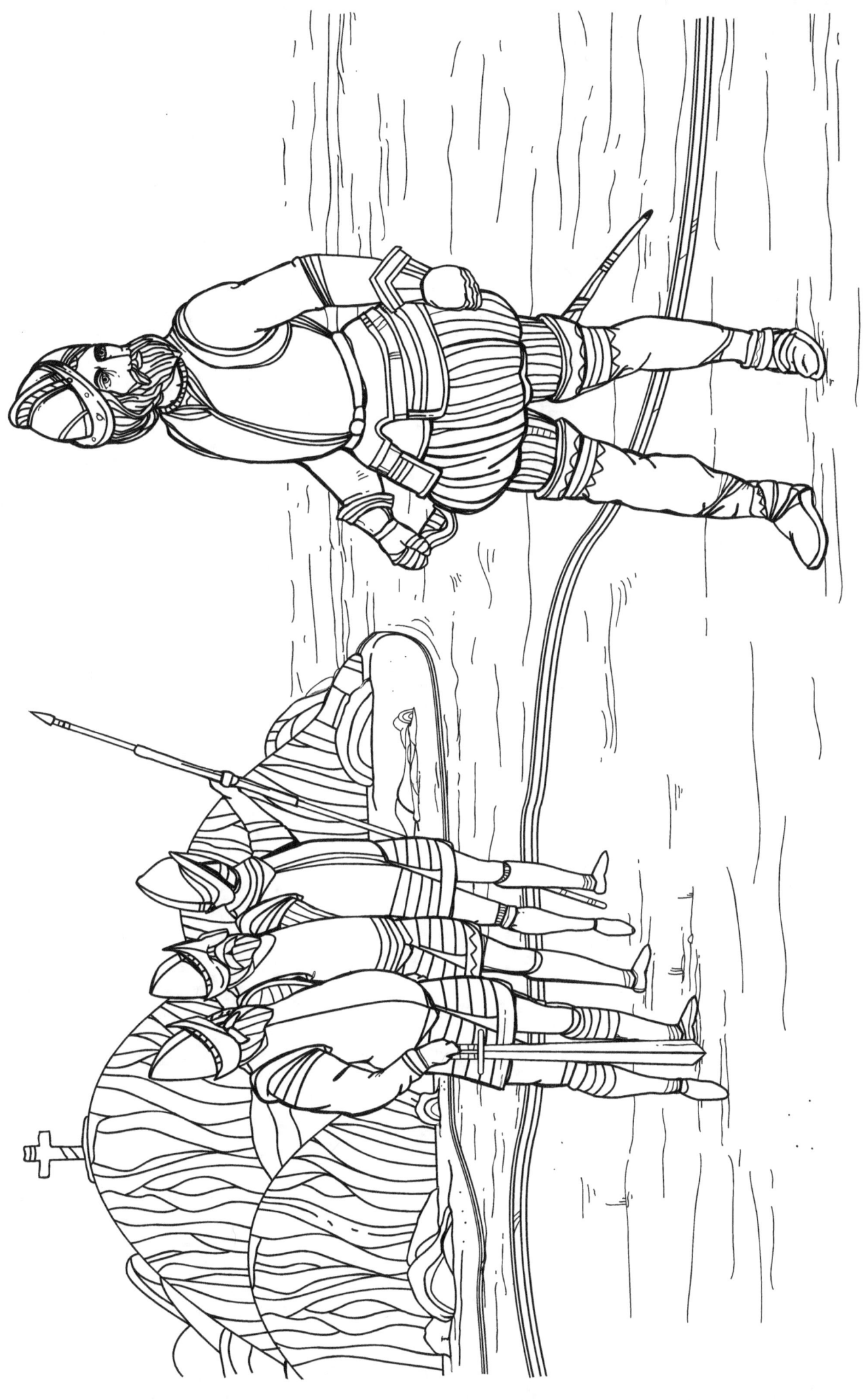

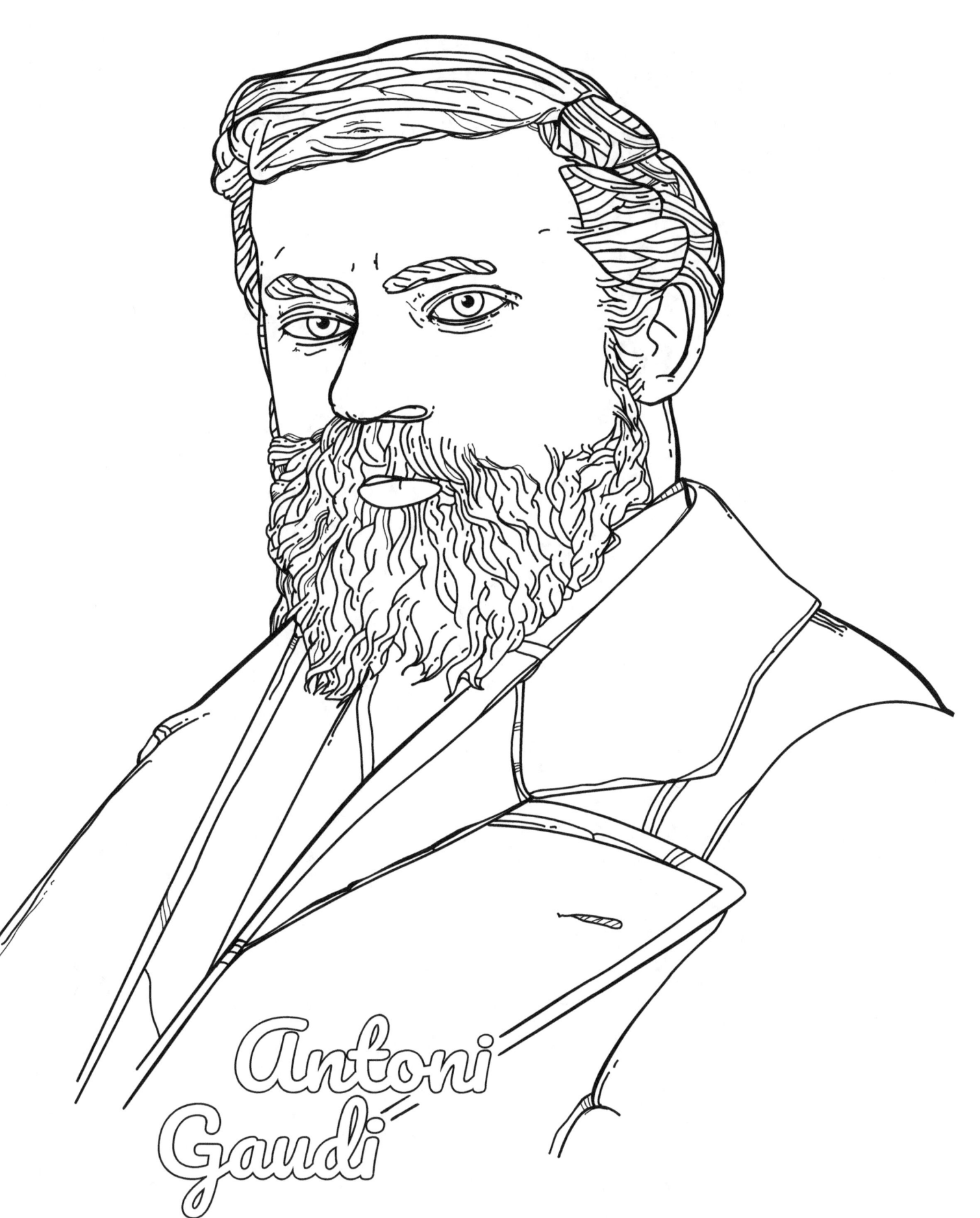

Antoni
Gaudí

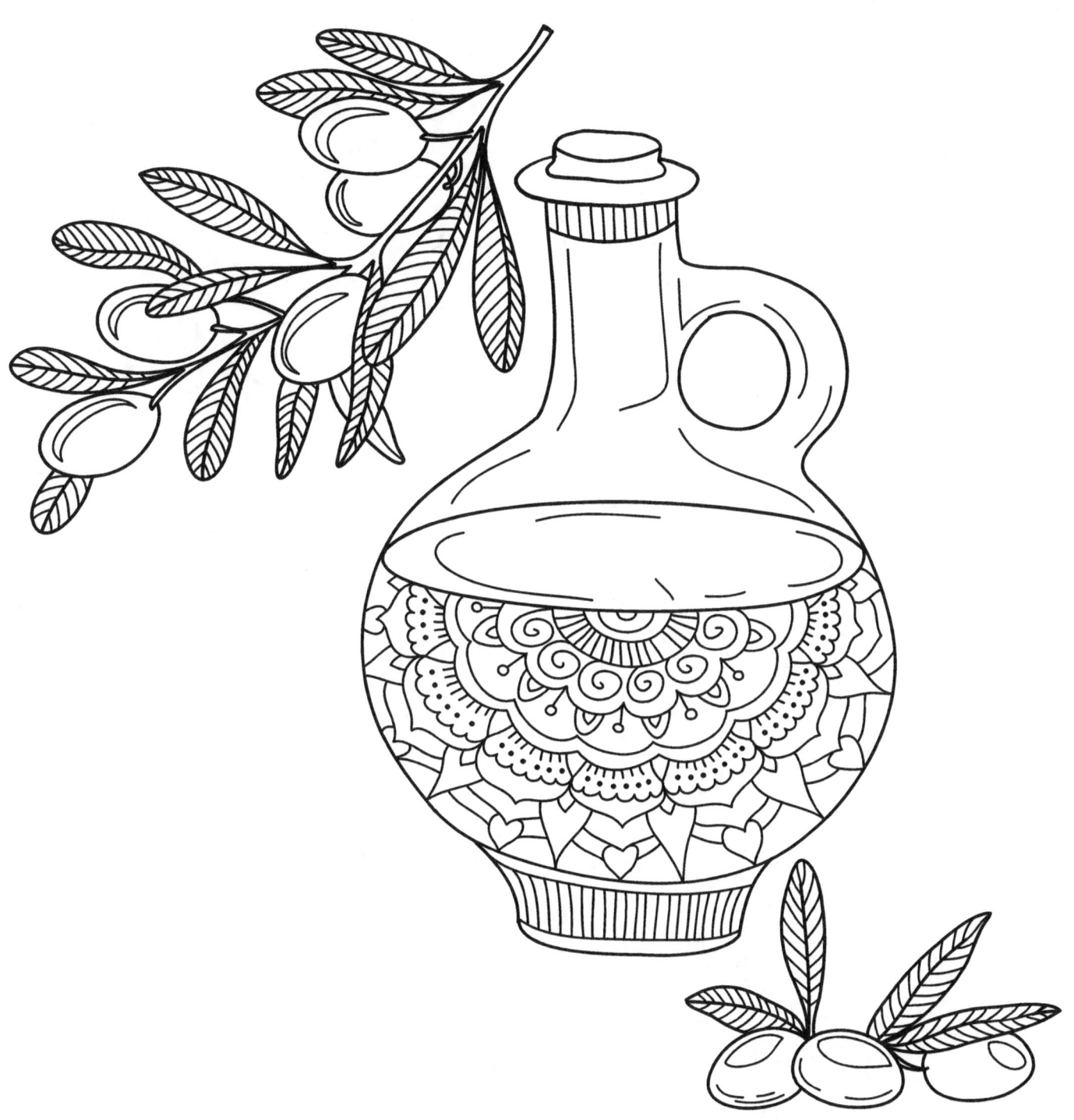

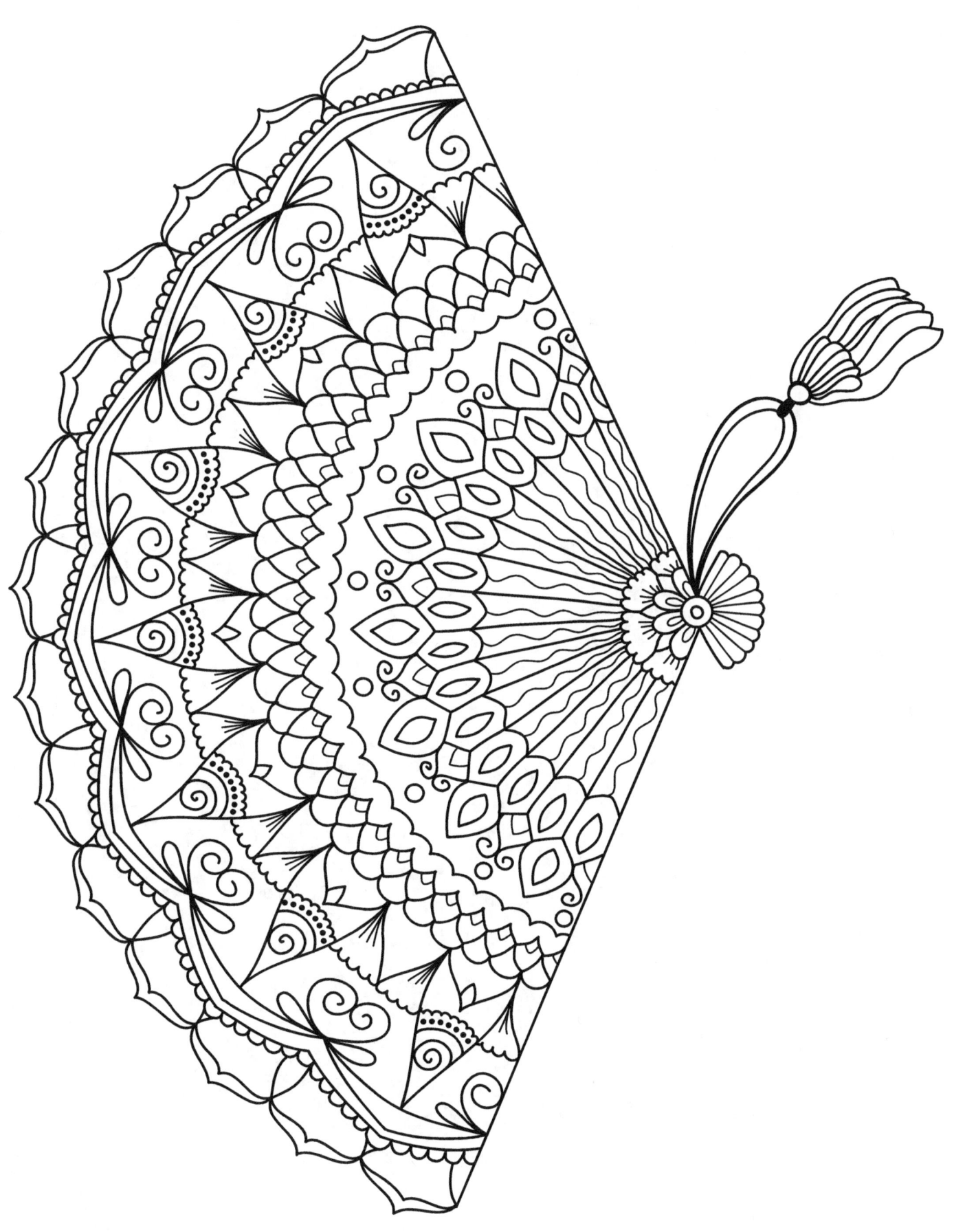

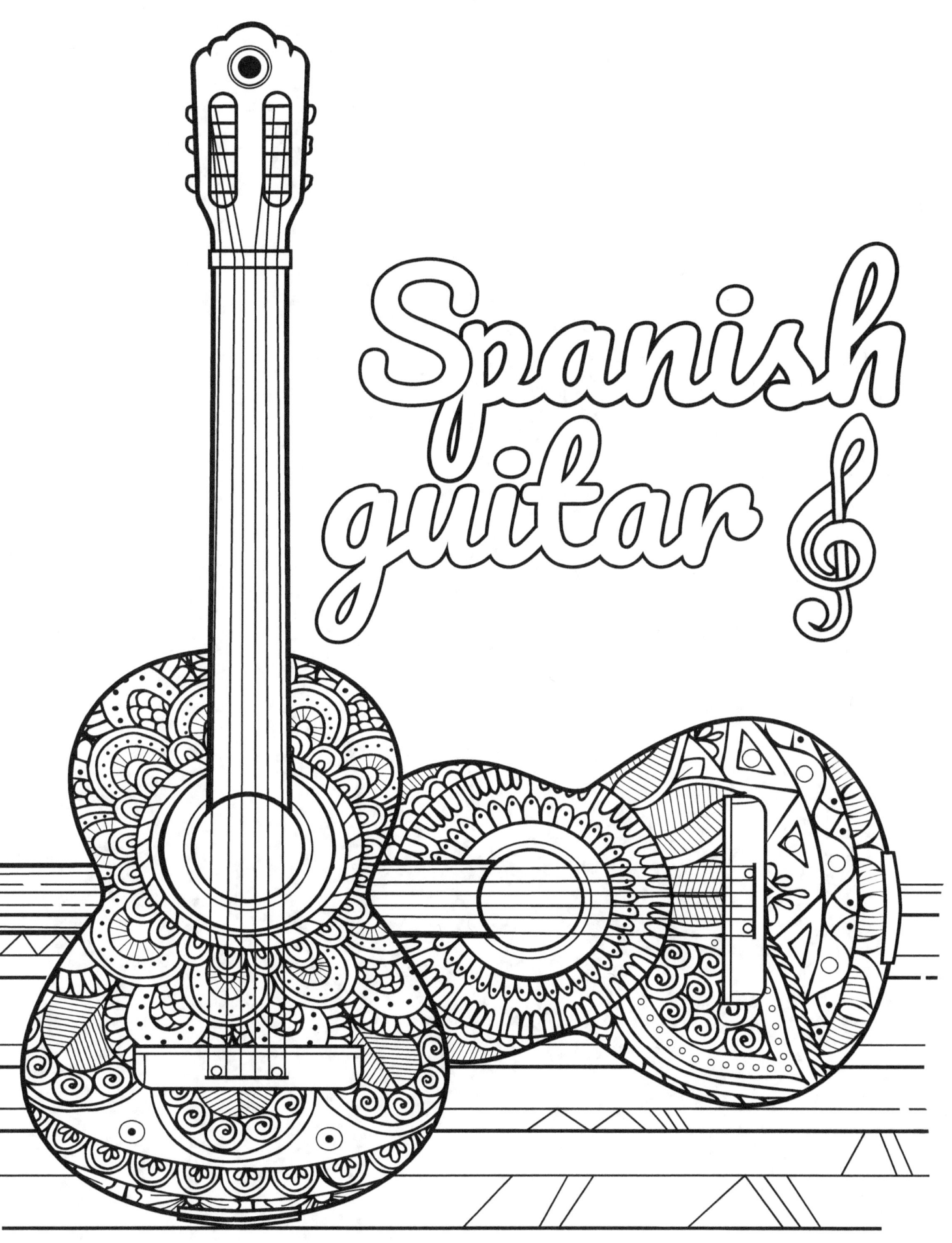

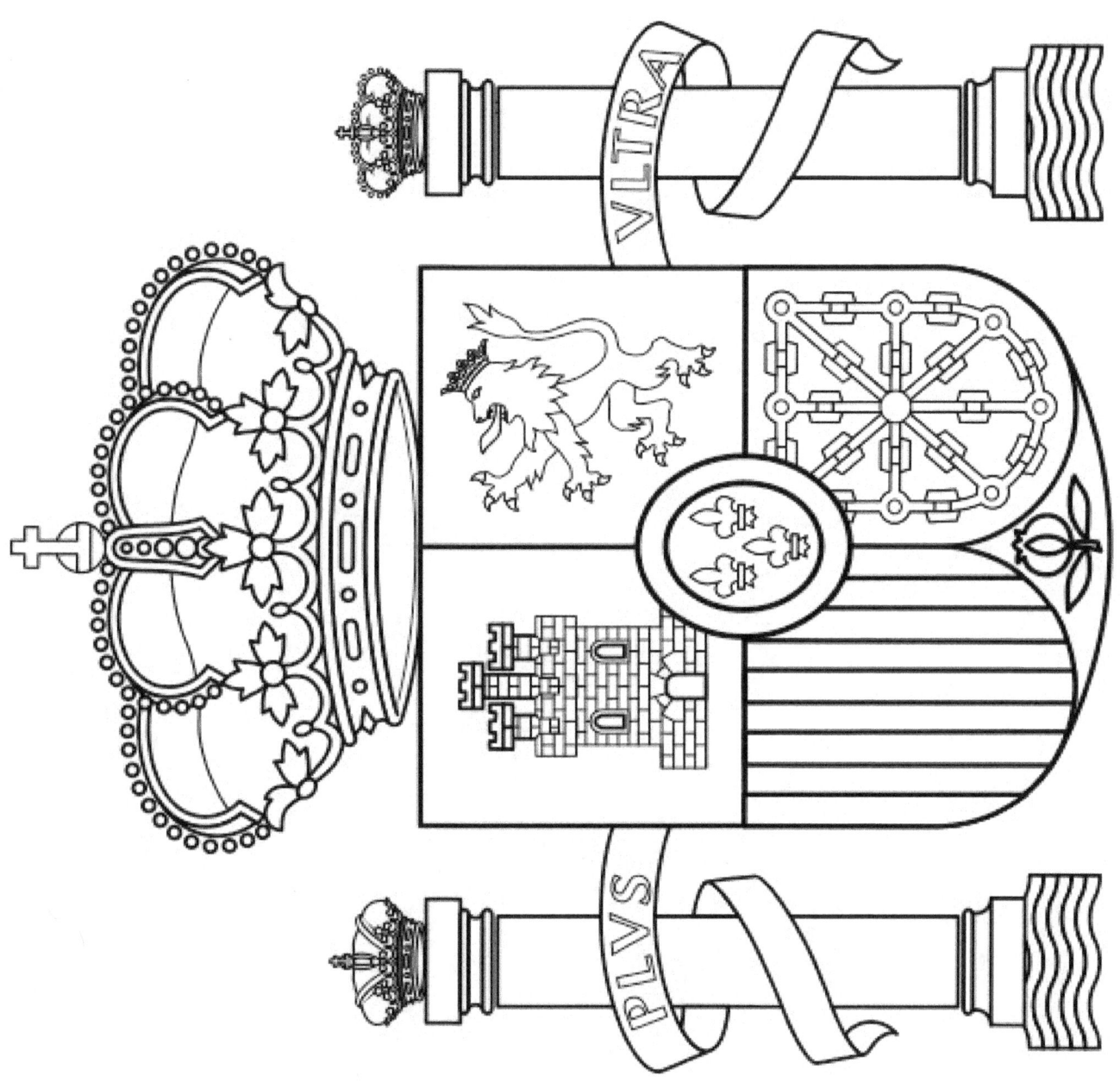

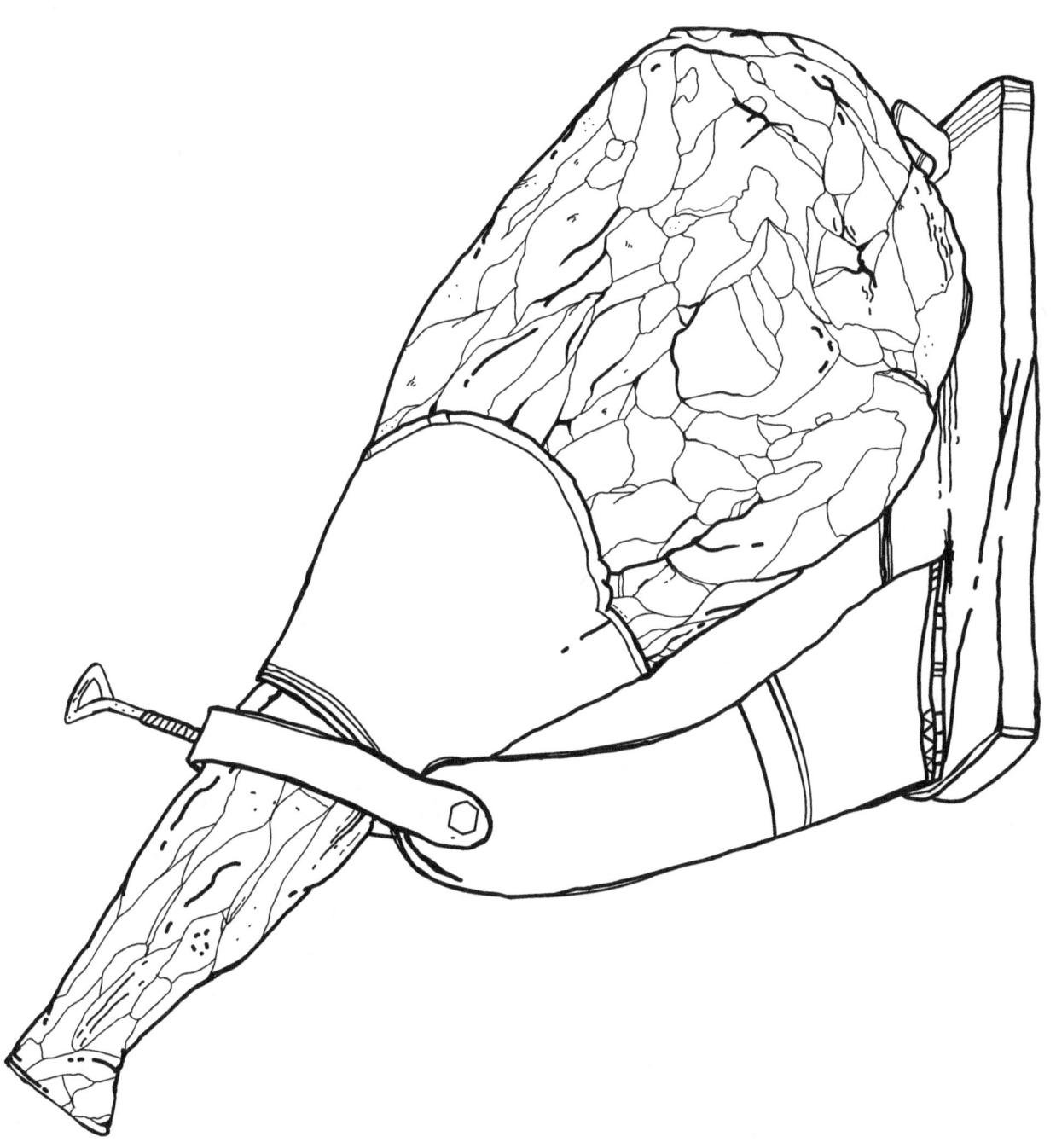

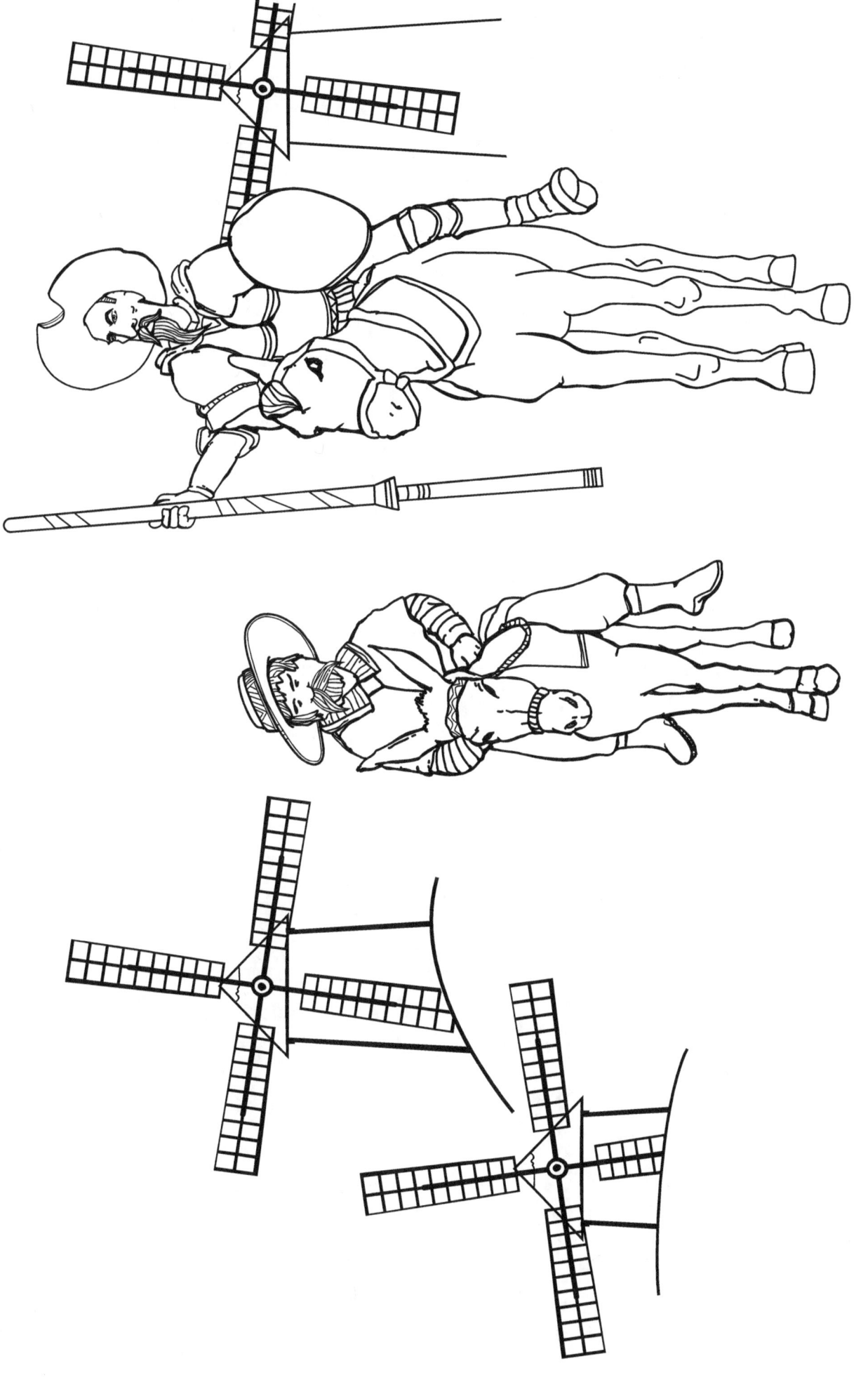

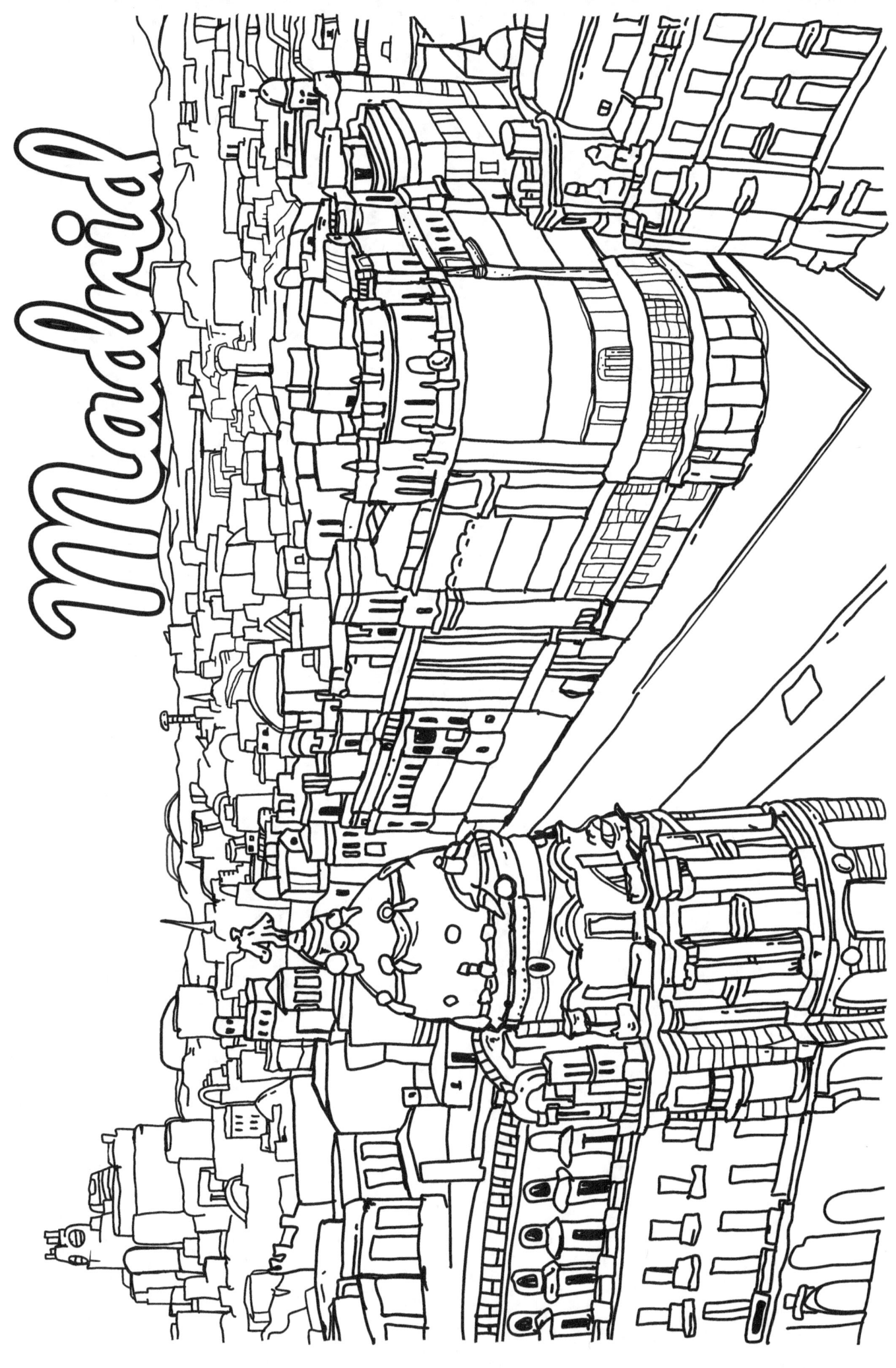

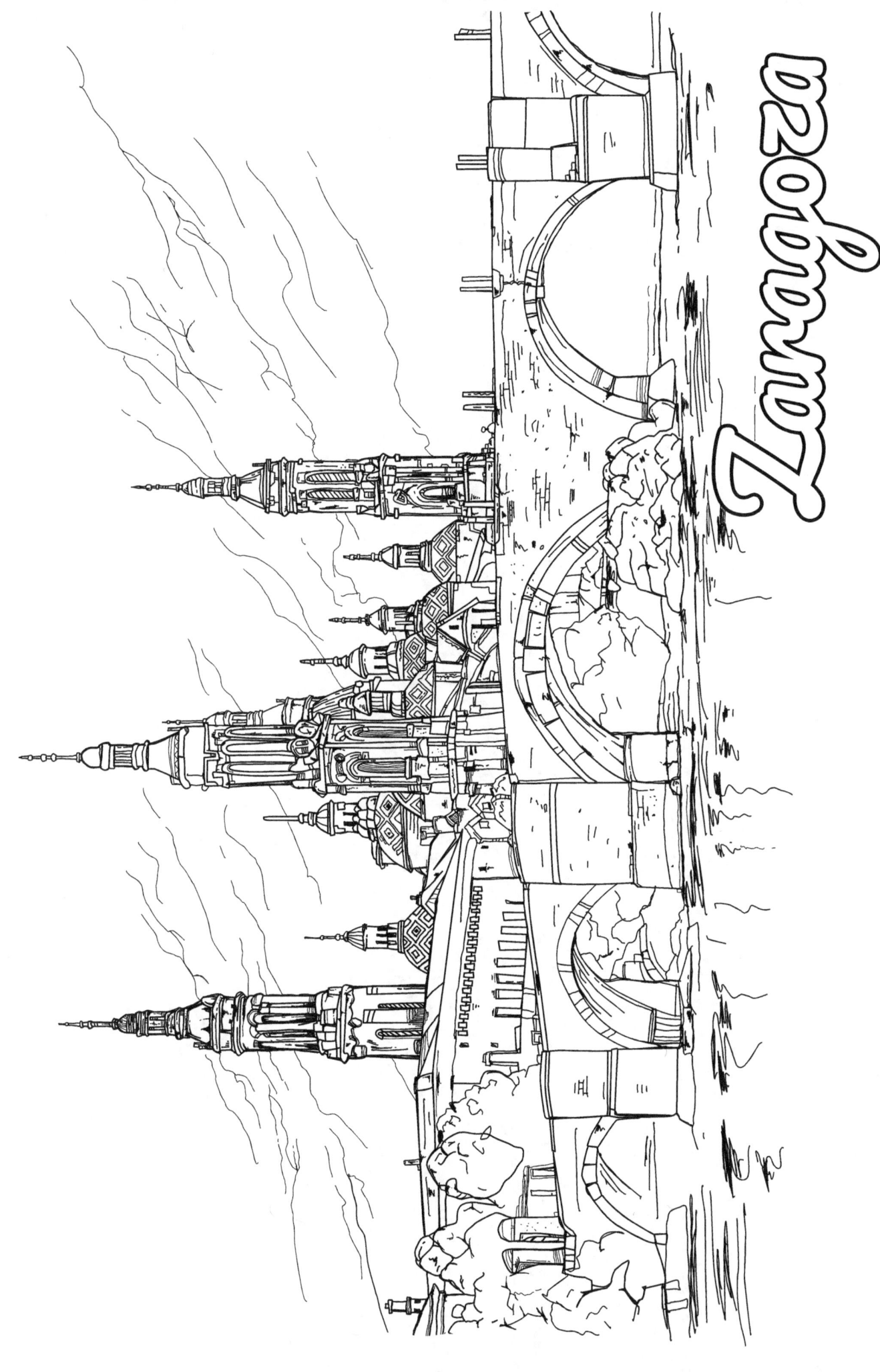

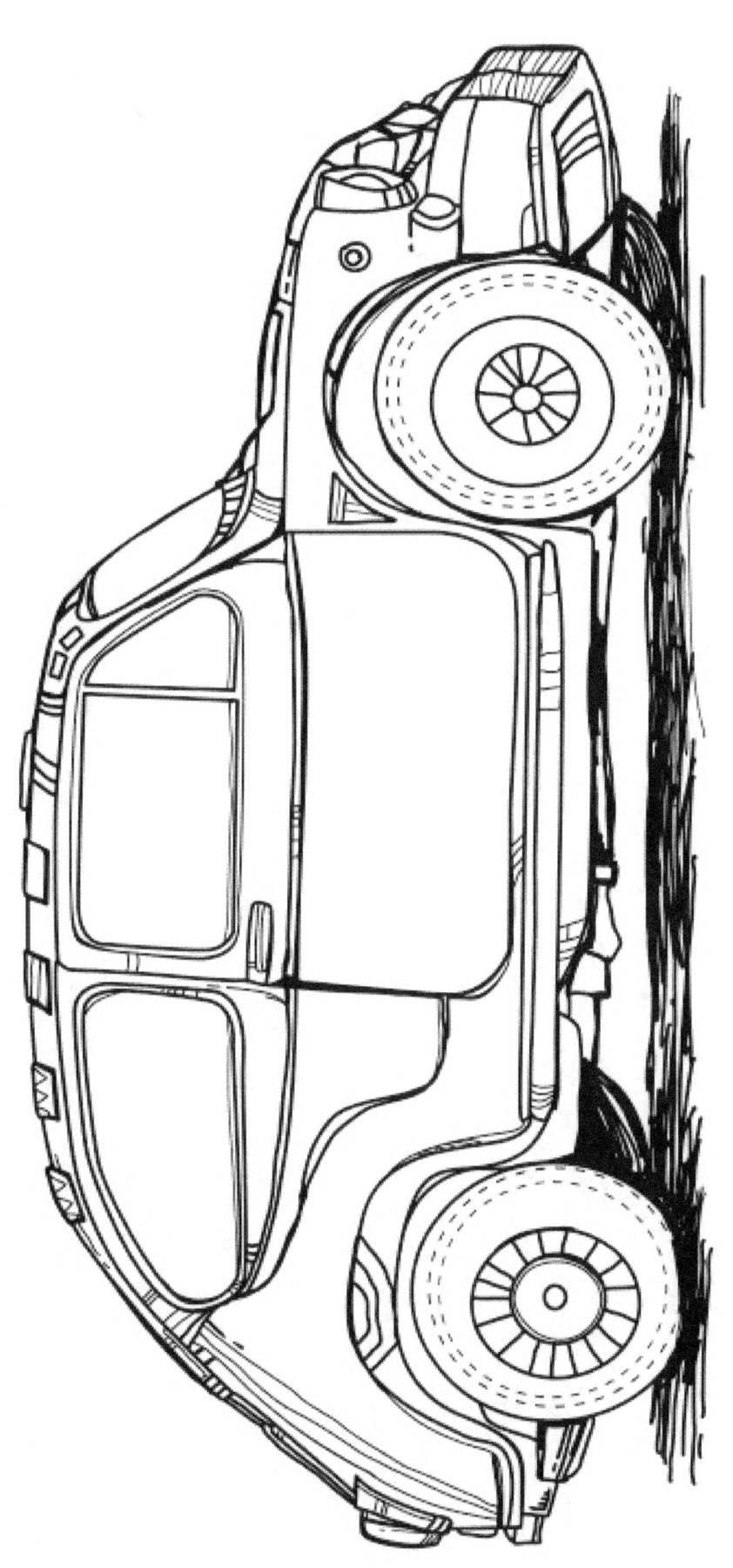

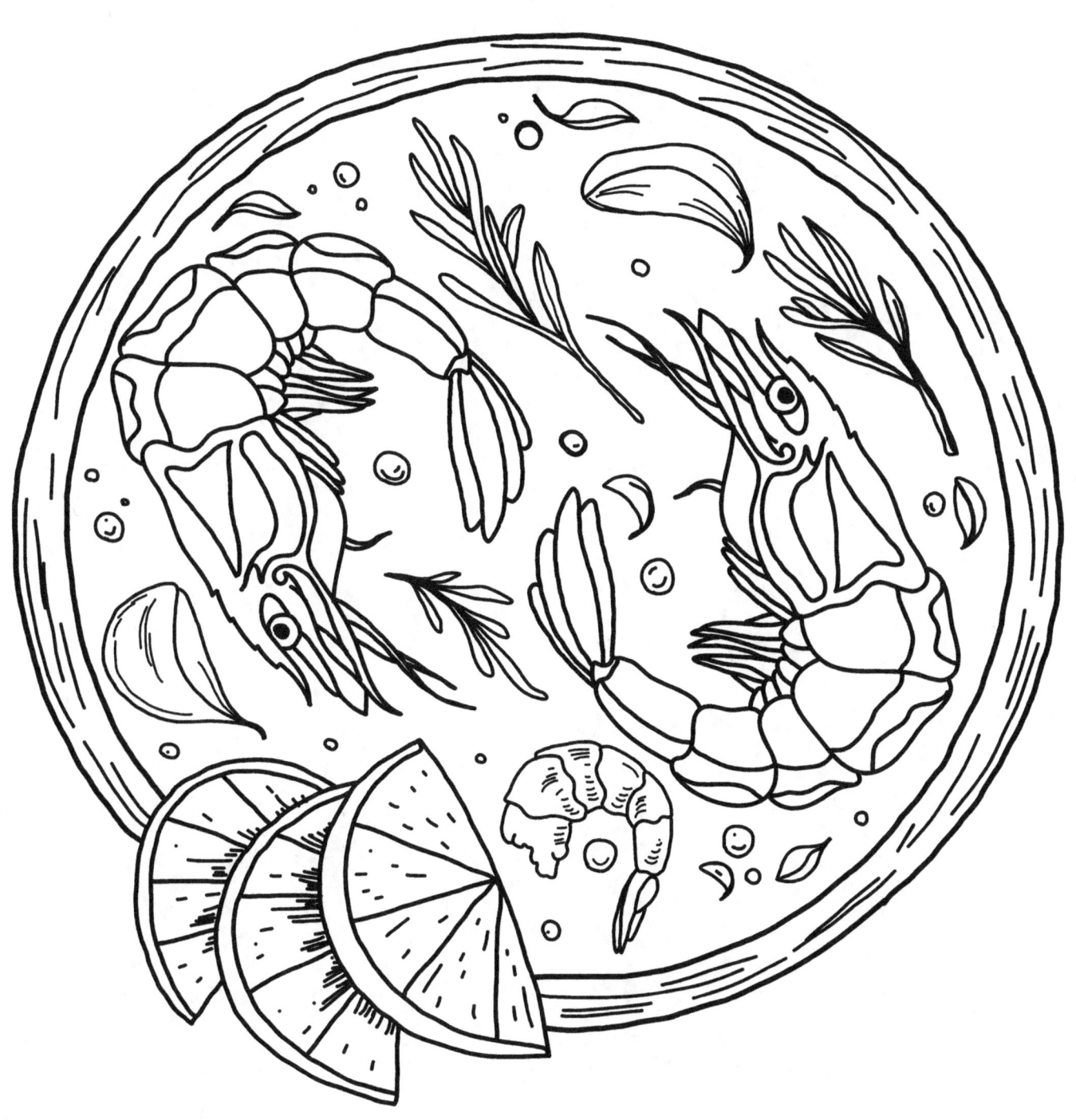

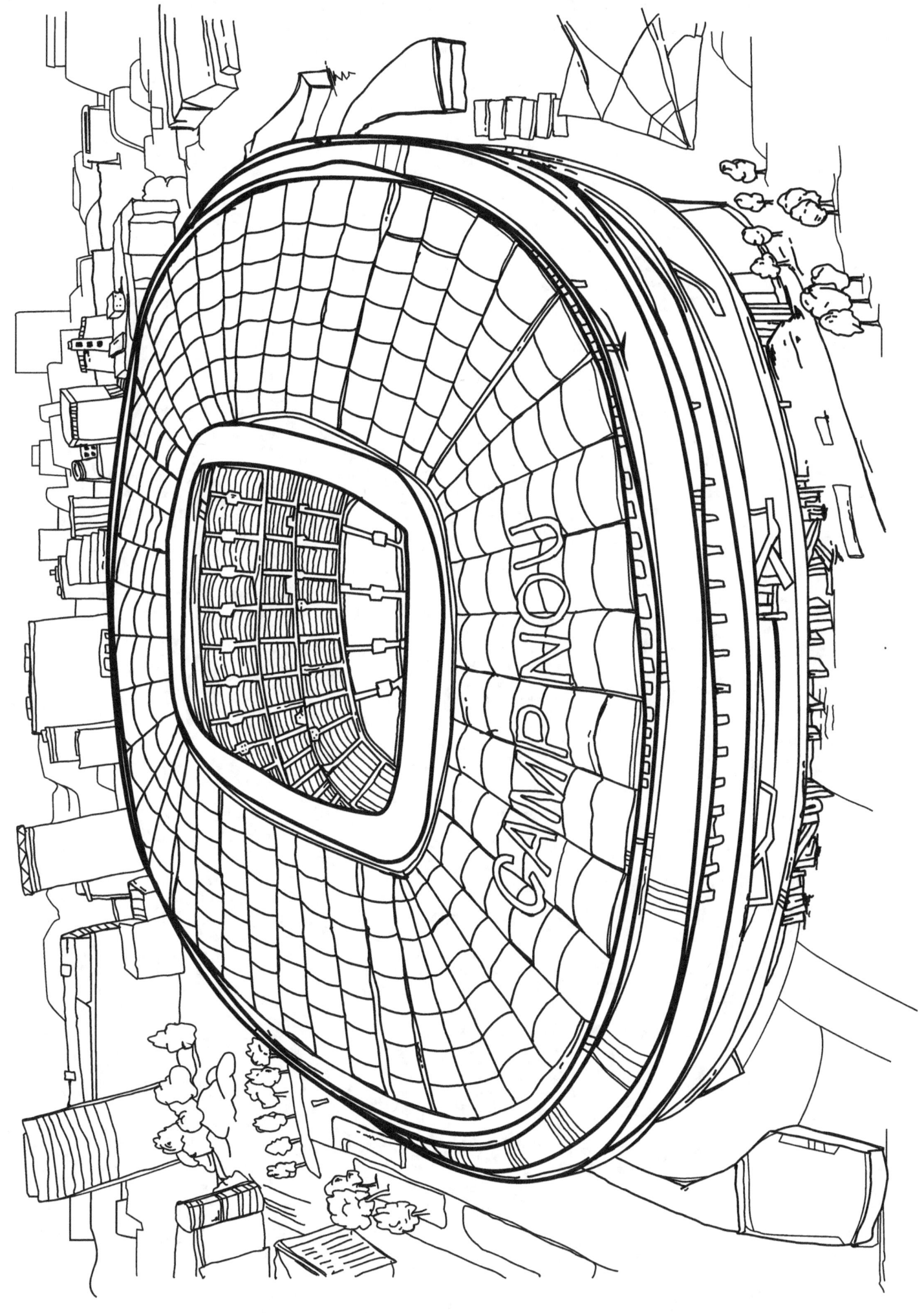

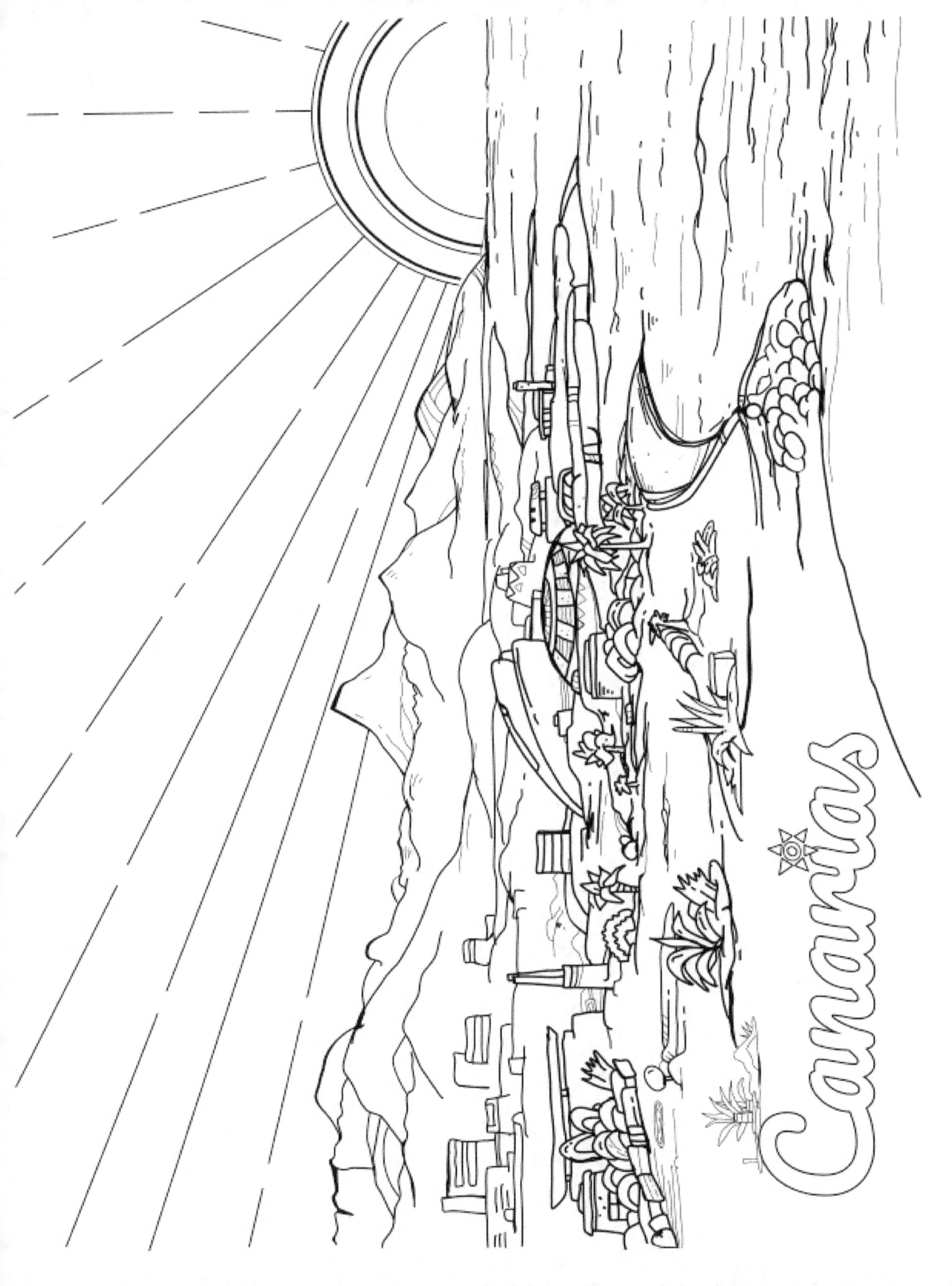

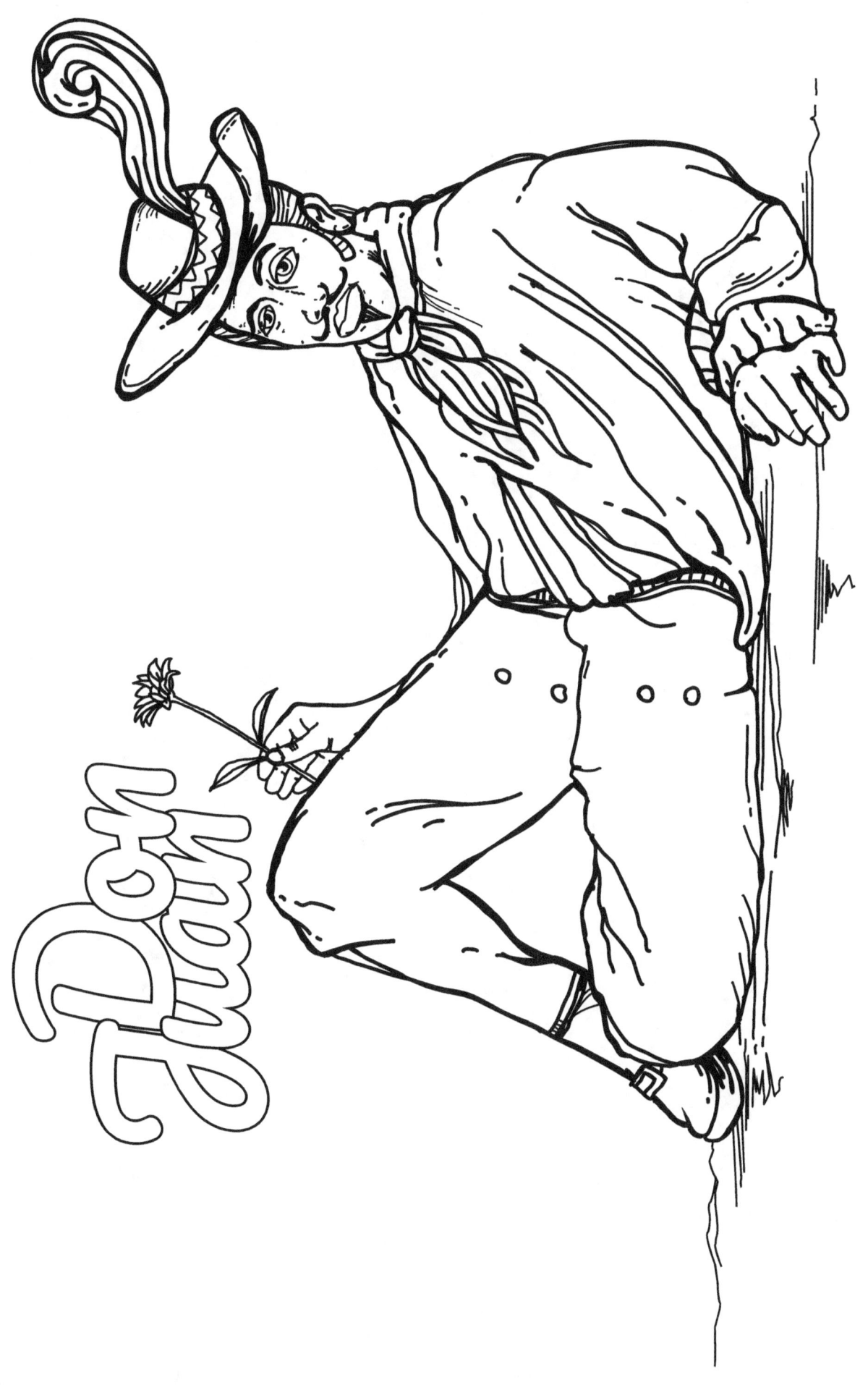

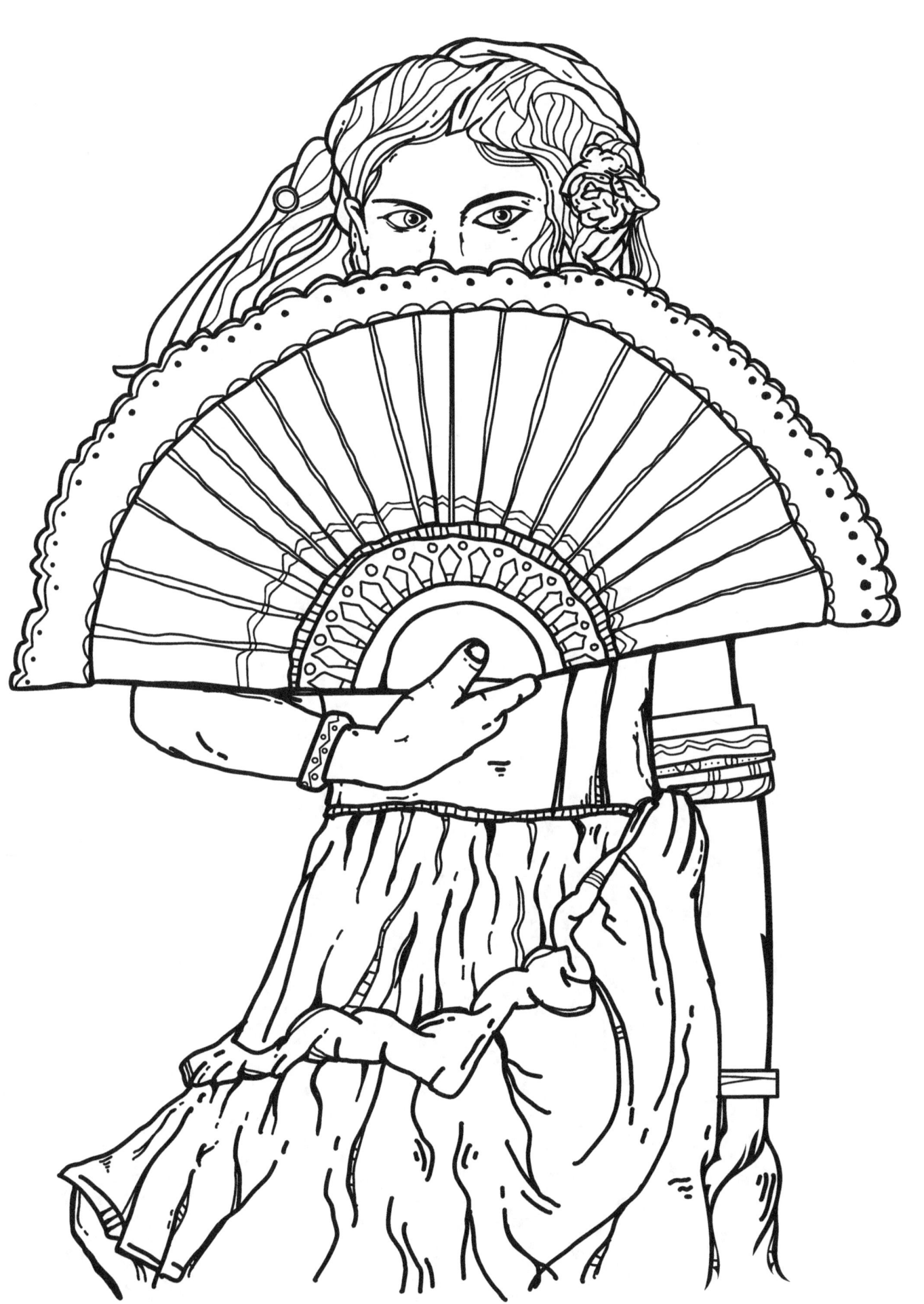

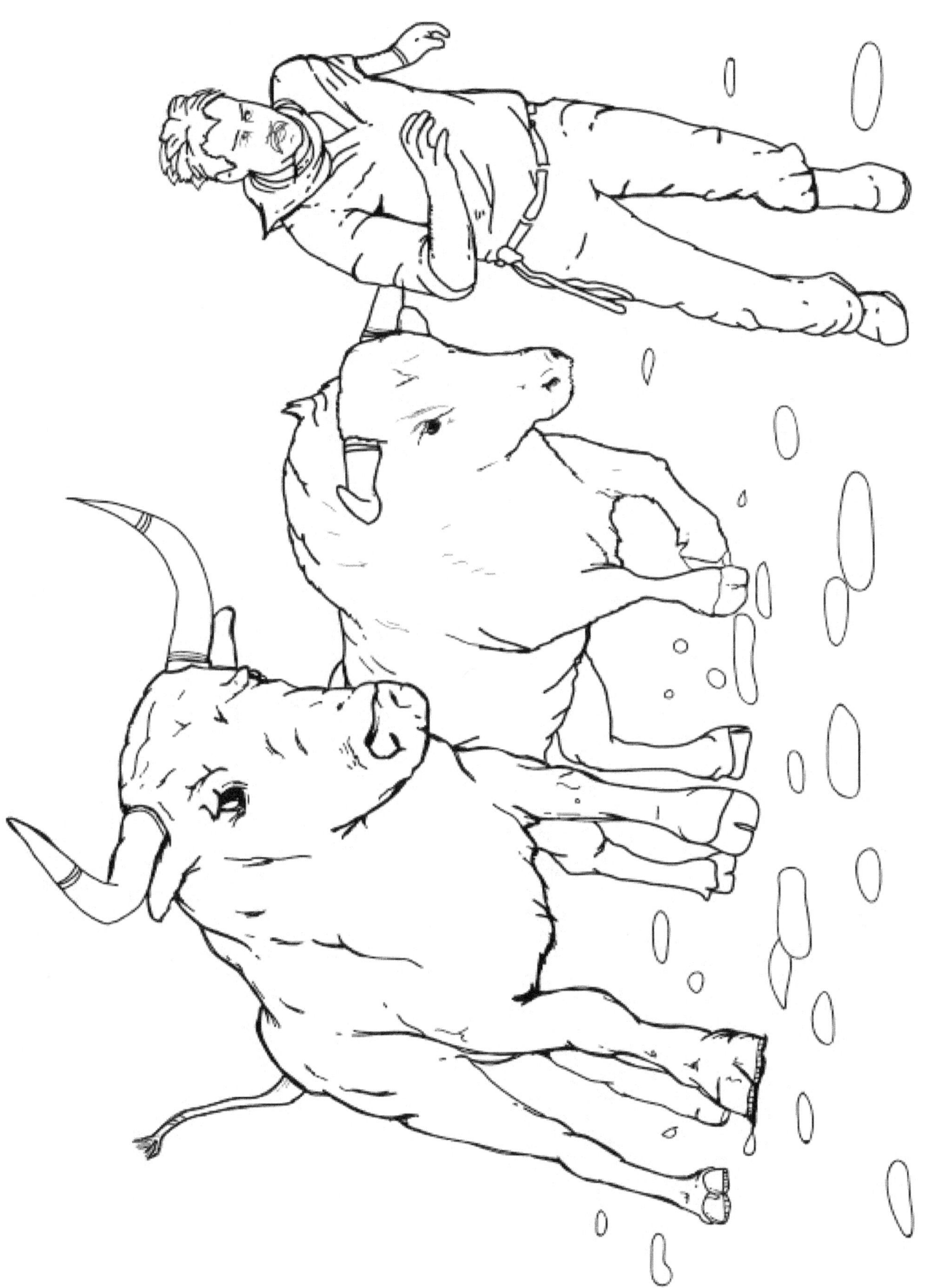

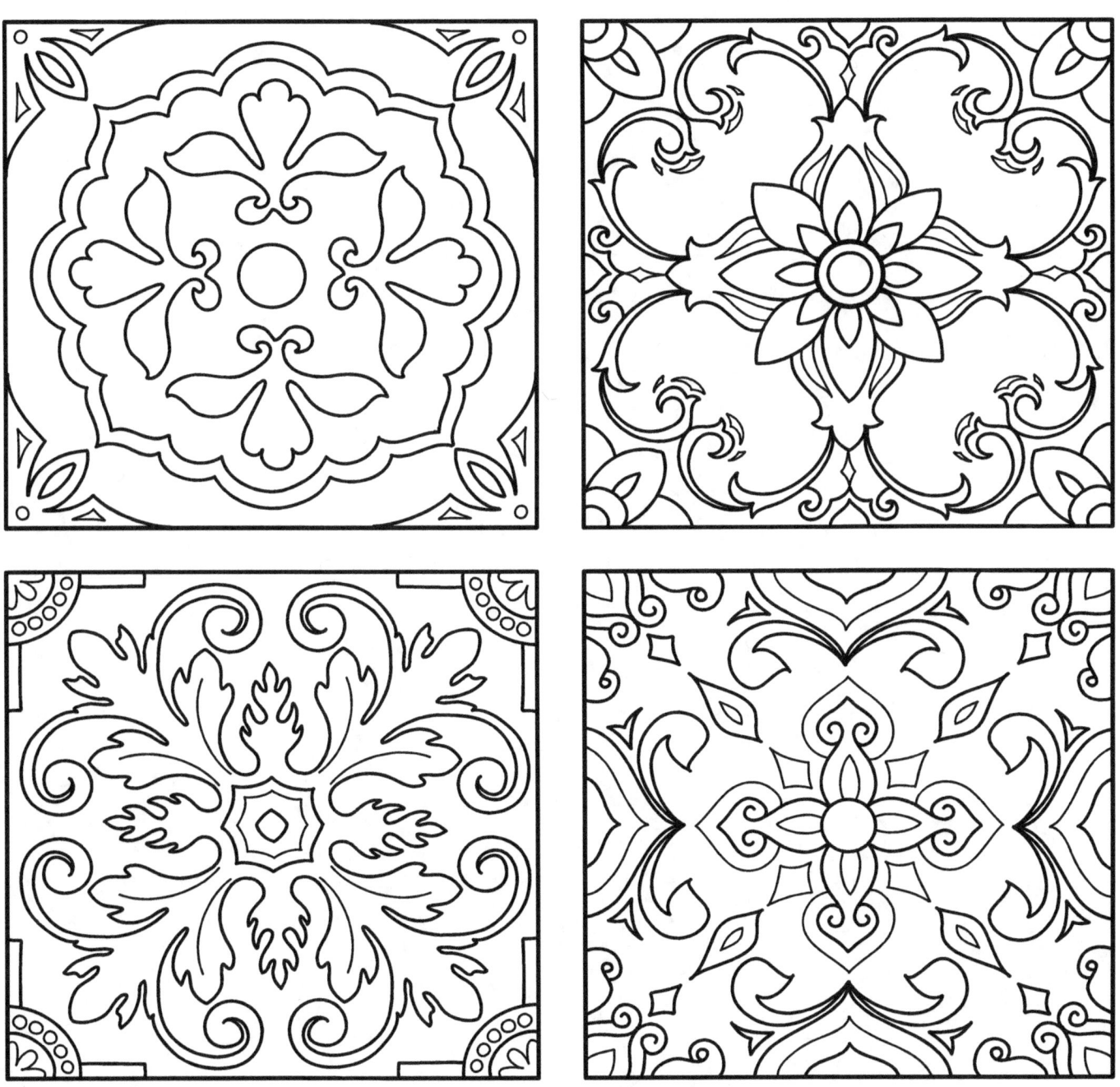

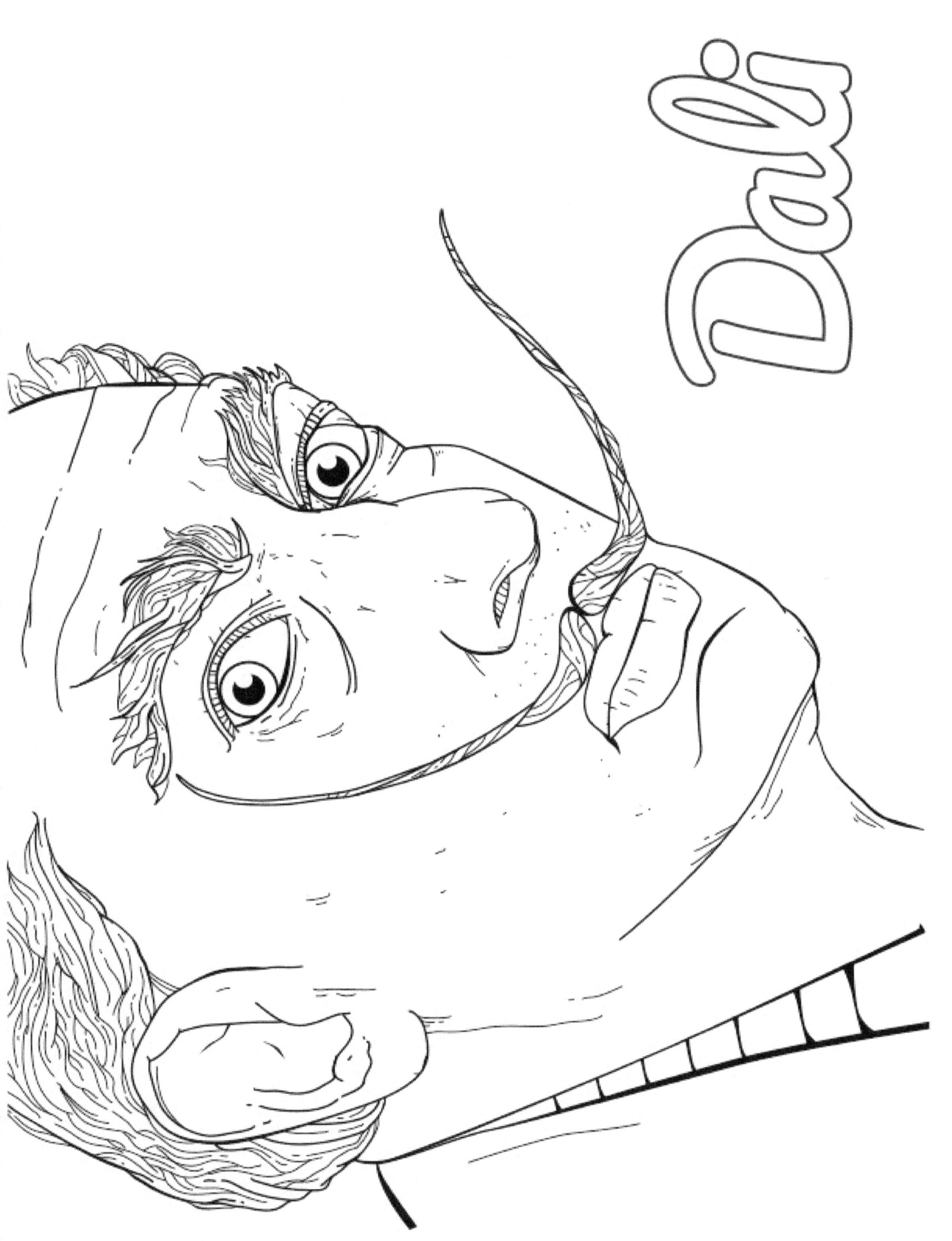

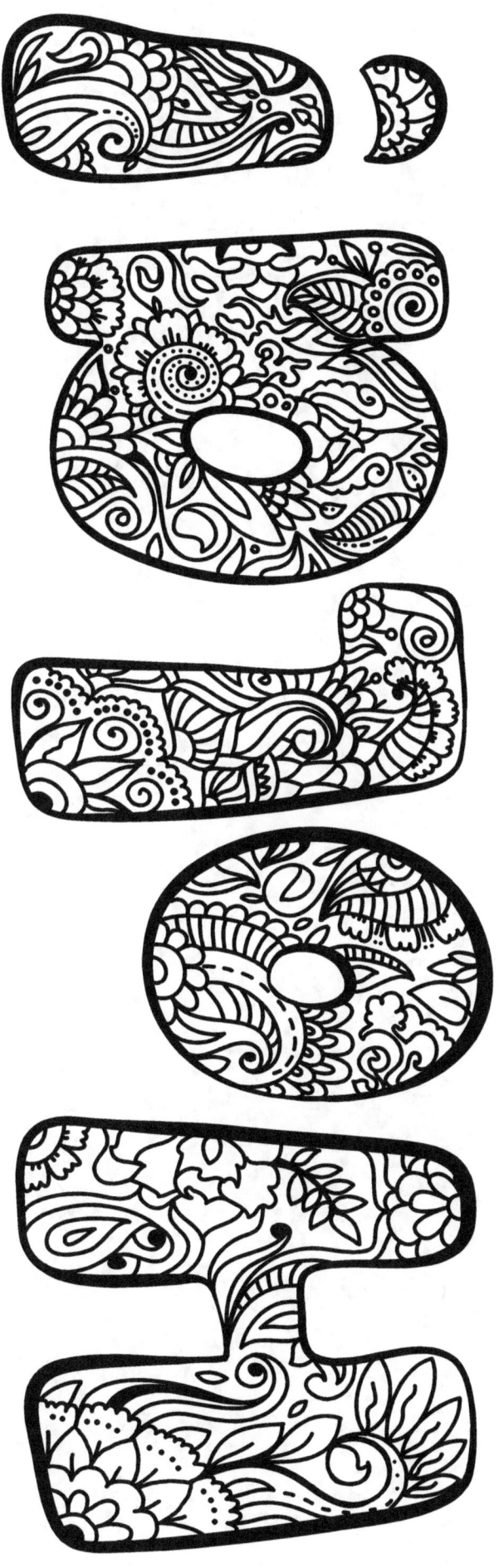

Thank you for purchasing this book.

If you would like to know more about Aryla Publishing Books please visit:-

www.ArylaPublishing.com

Or follow us on
Facebook
Twitter
Instagram
for *free promotions*

@arylapublishing

We would love to know what you think of this book so please leave us a review.

Have a wonderful day ☺

Other Coloring Books from Aryla Publishing

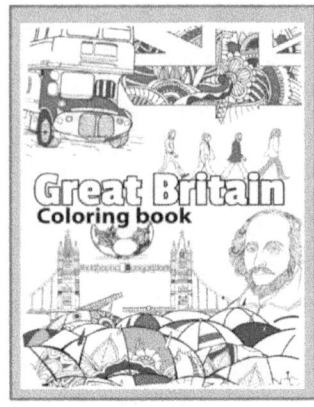

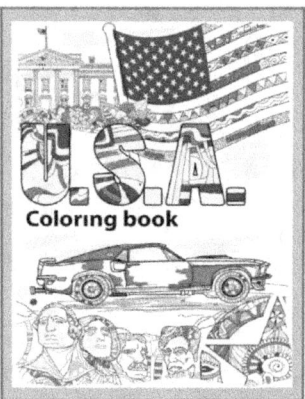

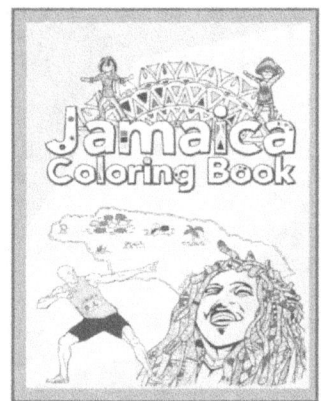

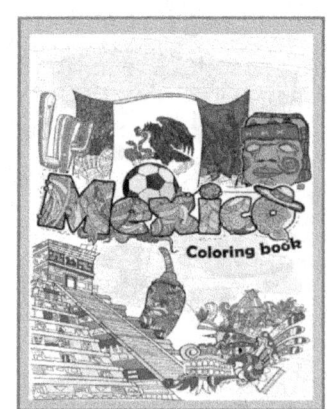

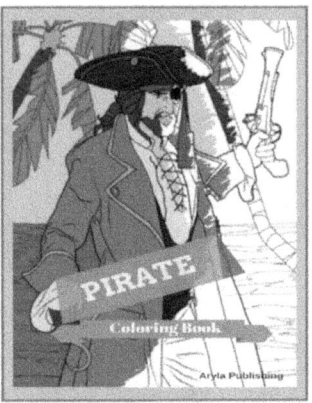

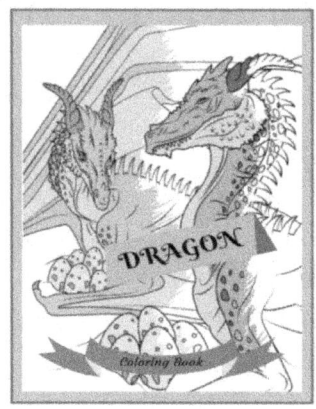

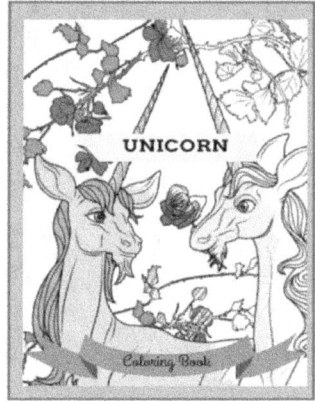

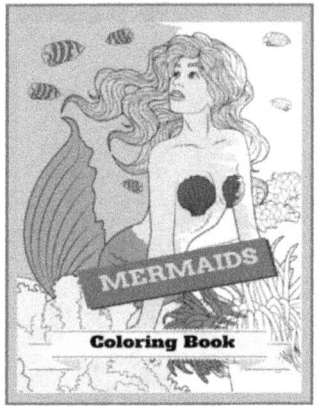

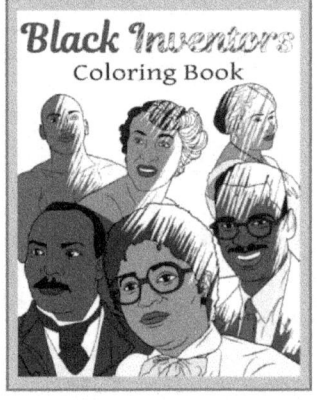

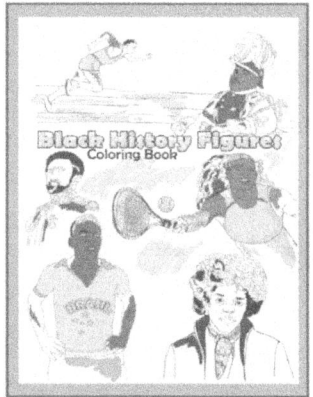

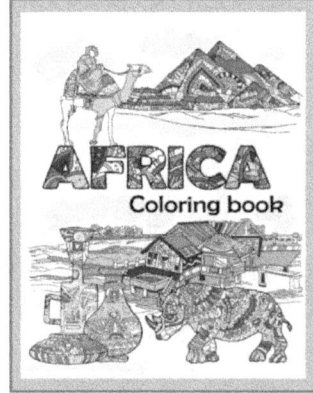

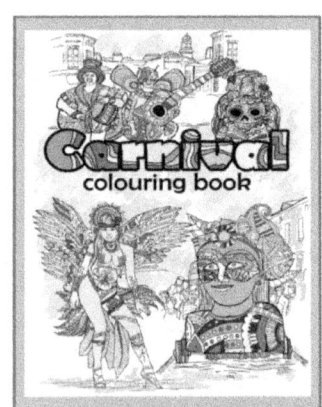

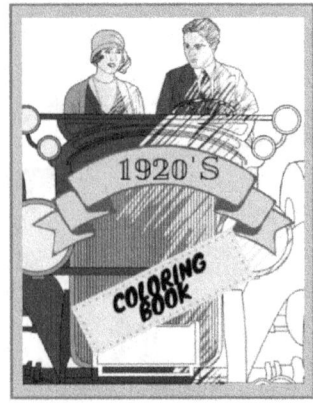

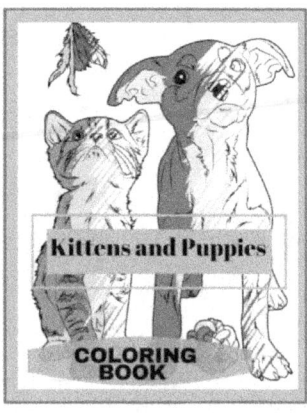

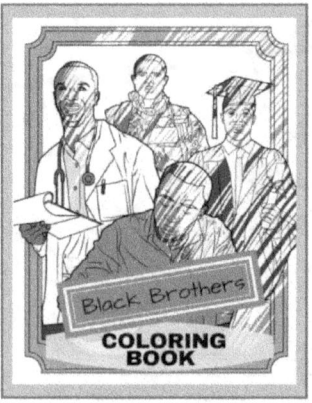

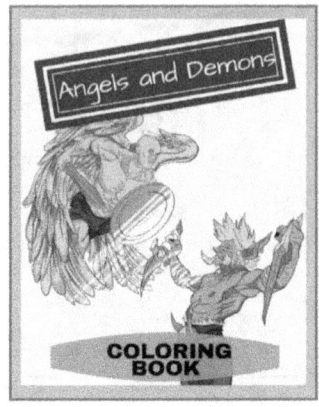

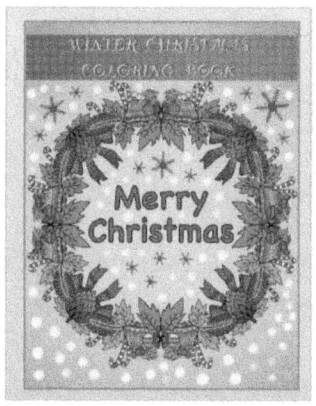
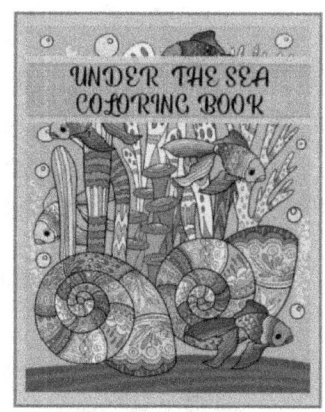
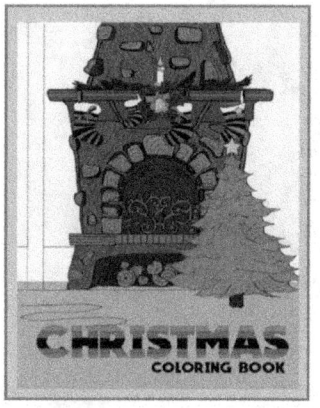
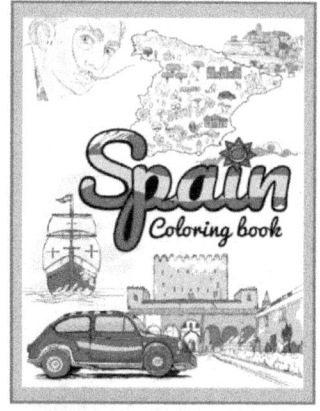
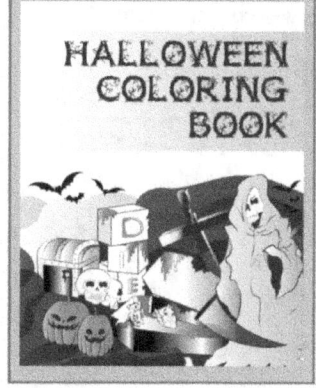
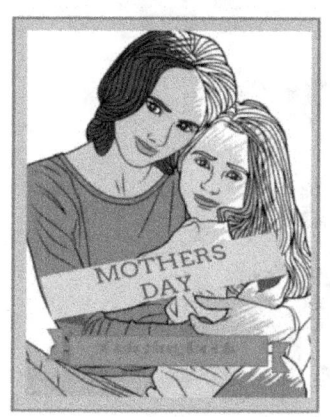
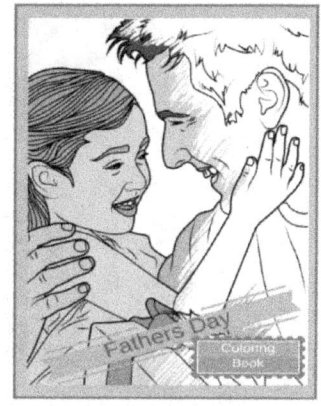
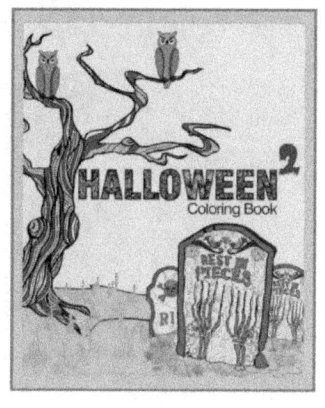
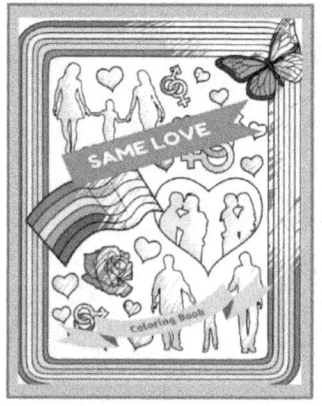
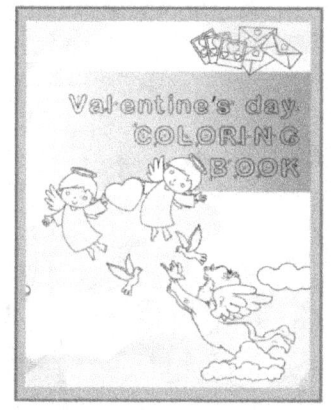
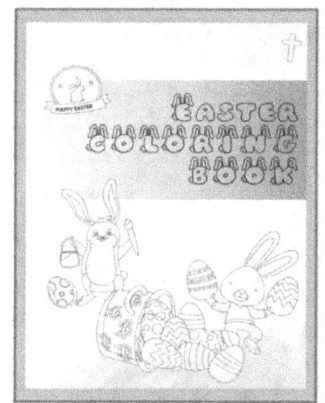
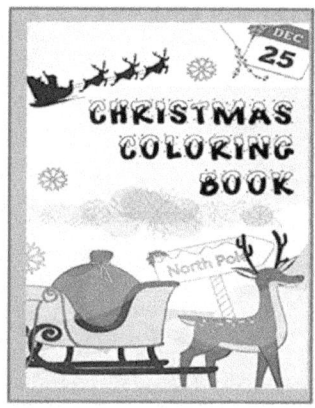
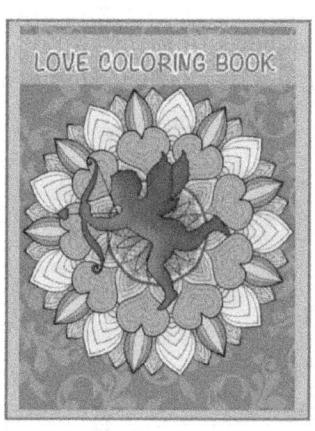
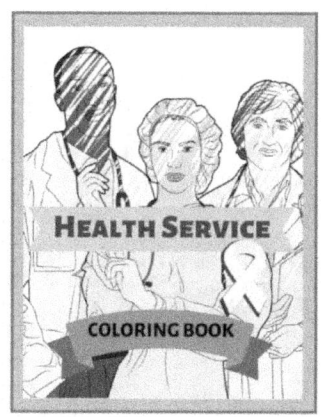
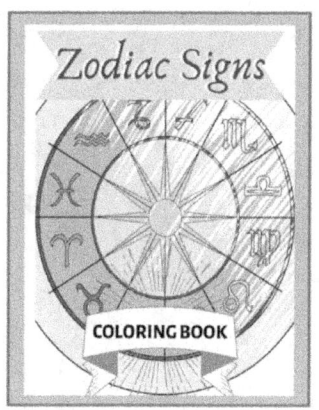
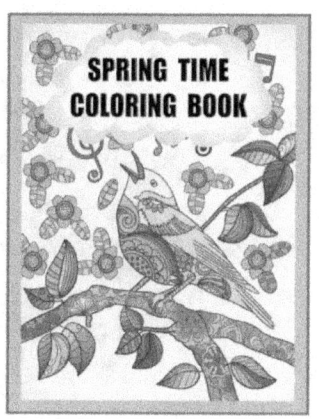

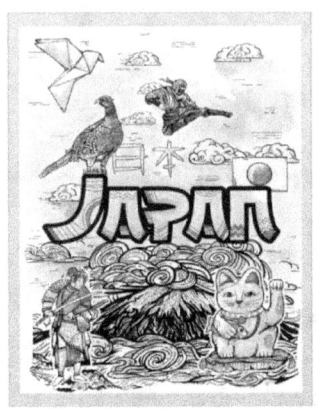

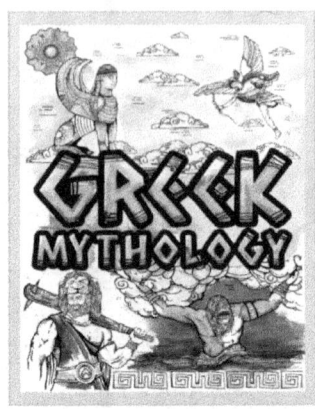

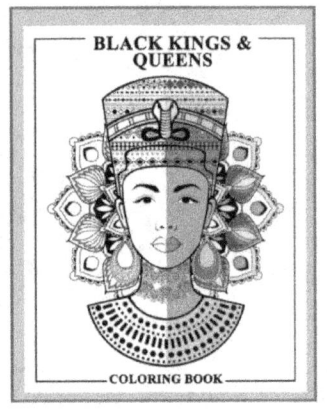

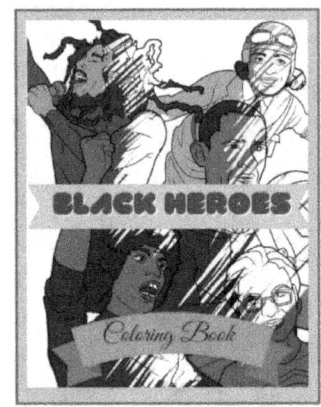

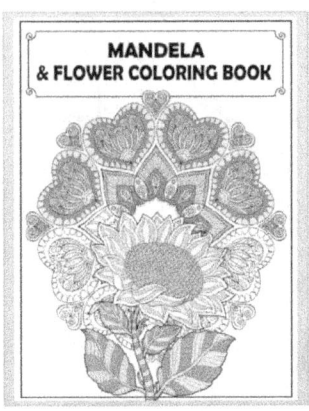

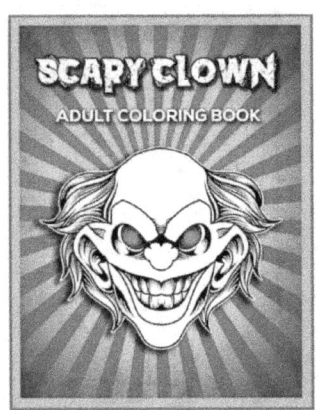

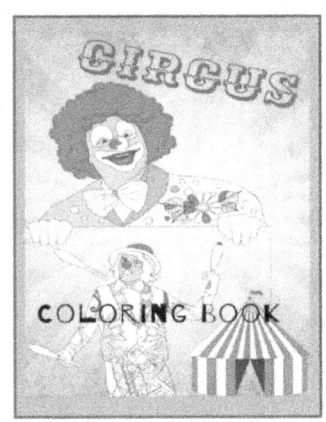

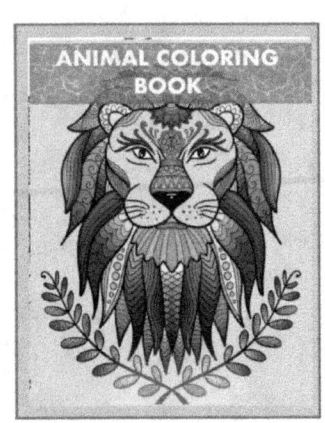

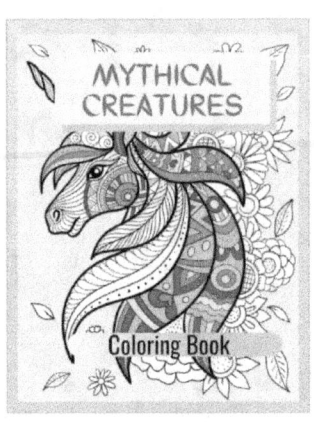

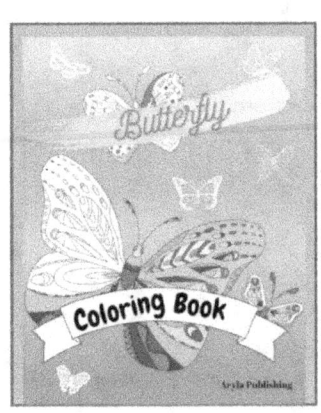

Color In Fun
Kids Books

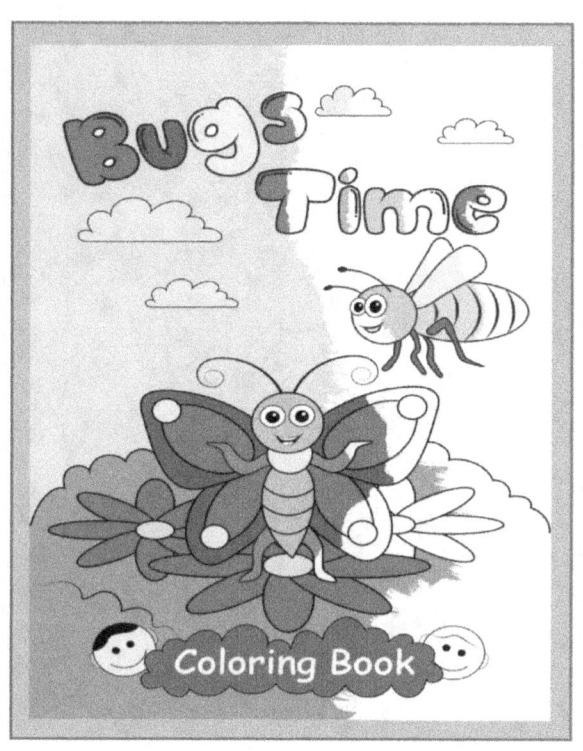

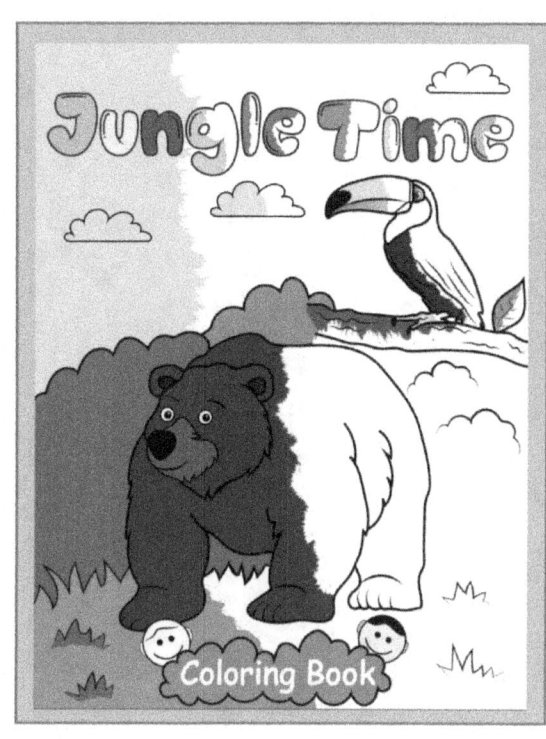

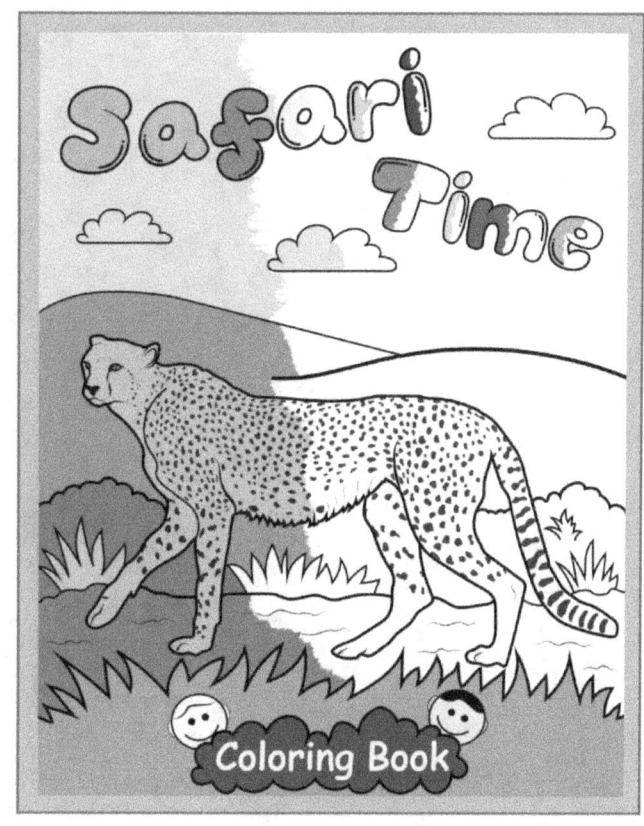

Visit **www.ArylaPublishing.com**
to find out about all new releases.

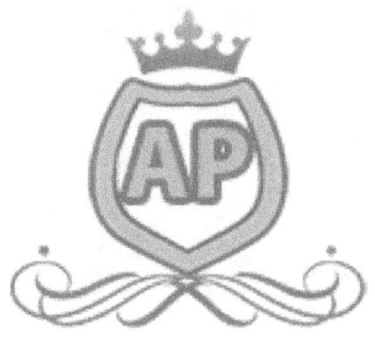

Follow us @arylapublishing on Twitter Instagram & Facebook

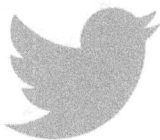  

Search for Aryla Publishing on

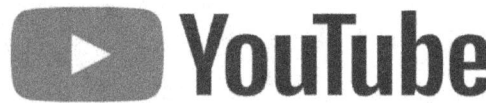 YouTube

Check out our <u>Book Trailers</u>

<u>*Subscribe*</u> *to keep up to date with new releases!*

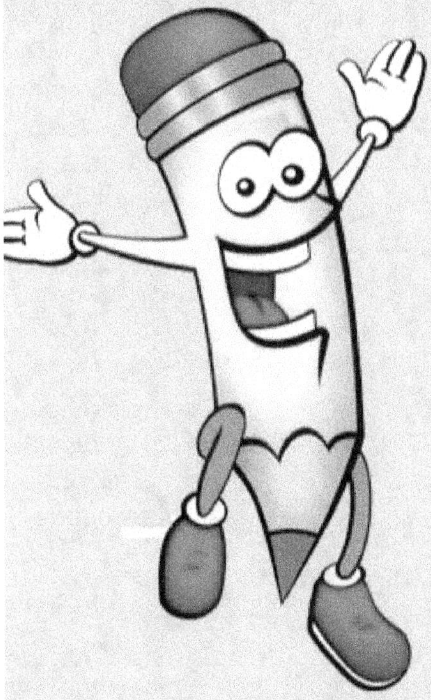

WE WOULD LOVE YOUR FEEDBACK

PLEASE LEAVE REVIEW AT:-

https://bit.ly/spainreview

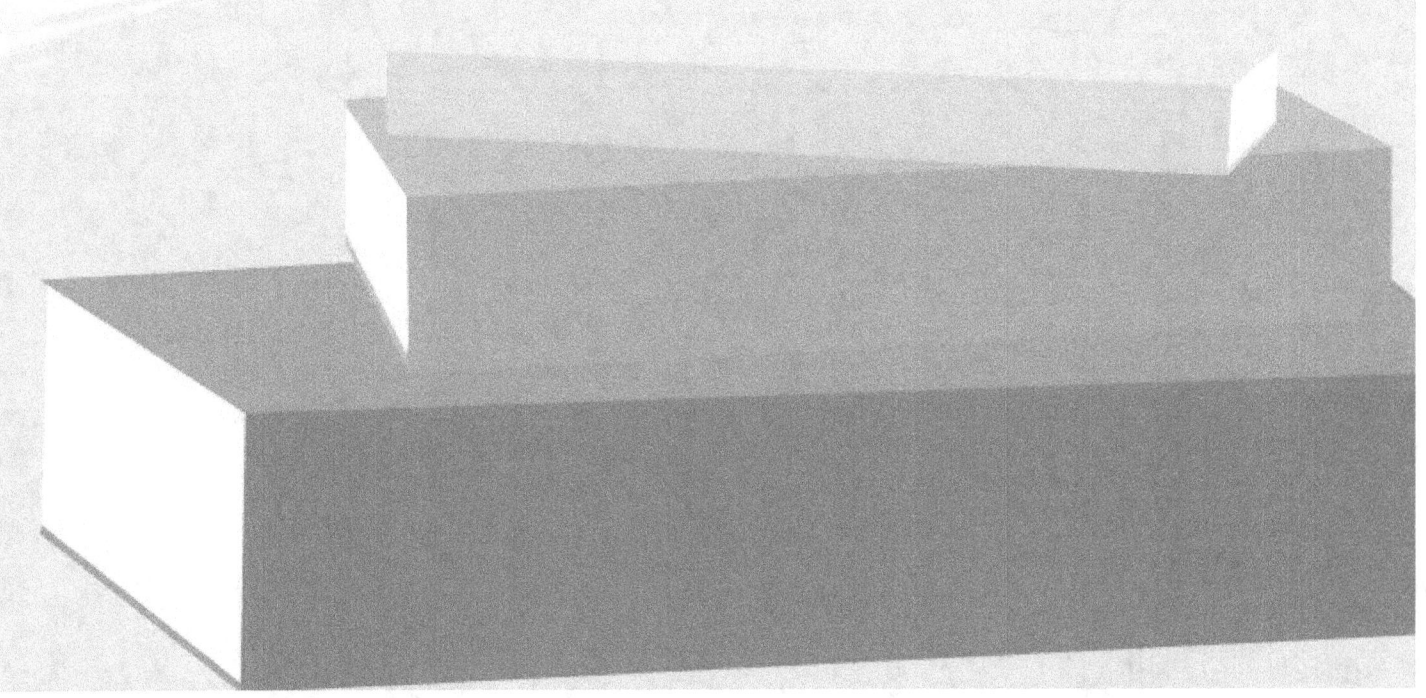

www.ingramcontent.com/pod-product-compliance
Lightning Source LLC
Chambersburg PA
CBHW082014230526
45468CB00022B/2199